Minimalist Life

How to Declutter Your Life and Function at Your Best

Nia Asha

© Copyright 2019 - All rights reserved.

The content contained within this book may not be reproduced, duplicated or transmitted without direct written permission from the author or the publisher.

Under no circumstances will any blame or legal responsibility be held against the publisher, or author, for any damages, reparation, or monetary loss due to the information contained within this book, either directly or indirectly.

Legal Notice:

This book is copyright protected. It is only for personal use. You cannot amend, distribute, sell, use, quote or paraphrase any part, or the content within this book, without the consent of the author or publisher.

Disclaimer Notice:

Please note the information contained within this document is for educational and entertainment purposes only. All effort has been executed to present accurate, up to date, reliable, complete information. No warranties of any kind are declared or implied. Readers acknowledge that the author is not engaging in the rendering of legal, financial, medical or professional advice. The content within this book has been derived from various sources. Please consult a licensed professional before attempting any techniques outlined in this book.

By reading this document, the reader agrees that under no circumstances is the author responsible for any losses, direct or indirect, that are incurred as a result of the use of information contained within this document, including, but not limited to, errors, omissions, or inaccuracies.

Table of Contents

Book Description: Minimalist Life 1

Introduction.. 2

Chapter 1 The Act of Decluttering 4
    Where to Begin 4
    Why It Is Important 7
    How to Make It a Habit 9

Chapter 2 Ask Yourself What You Really Need 13
    Basic Needs 13
    Desires and Goals 16
    How to Let Go 18

Chapter 3 Learn How to Reuse 21
    Benefits of Reusing Items 21
    How to Become Savvier 24
    Ways to Create Less Waste 26

Chapter 4 Quality Over Quantity 30
    Why a Splurge Pays Off 30
    Investing in Your Future 33
    Avoiding Tempting Deals 35

Chapter 5 Keep What Makes You Happy 38
    Items That Hold Memories 39

How to Feel Satisfied with What You Have 41

Ways to Bring Meaning to Your Home 43

Chapter 6 How to Purge 47

How to Part with Things You No Longer Need 48

Getting Rid of Guilt 50

Make Purging a Regular Occurrence 52

Chapter 7 Replace Items You Already Own 55

How to Excel at Replacement 56

Treating Yourself to New Items 58

Maintaining Minimalism While Shopping 61

Chapter 8 Tips to Make Your Life More Efficient 64

Utilize Technology 65

Incorporate Organization 67

Make Final Decisions 69

Conclusion 72

Bonus Material: 75

Book: Minimalism; Beginners Guide to Minimalism 75

Check out our Other *AMAZING* Titles! 85

1. Mind Hacking; Learn the Secrets to Change Your Mind to Positivity in 20 Days 85

The Brain as a Computer 87

Mind Hacking for Positivity 89

2. Declutter Your Mind; Your Daily Guide to
Eliminate Stress, Stop Negative Thoughts and Anxiety Relief for a Happy Lifestyle 96

Reasons We Hang on To Clutter 99
Letting Go 102

References 105

Book Description: Minimalist Life

Minimalism is a lifestyle that promotes the idea that you can be happier with less. When everything has a purpose, you are able to feel more fulfilled in your daily life. The burden of clutter can stress you out, so minimalism teaches you how to get rid of what you no longer need while also teaching you how to keep your home clean and organized.

Through various minimalist techniques, you will learn how to take an assessment of what you already own, determining which items serve a purpose in your life. Thinking about what you truly need in your life to survive and what you want in order to be happy, you will then get rid of the items that are no longer useful.

This does not mean that you must throw everything that you own away, but simply repurpose or re-home the items so that they will be used. When something does need to be thrown away, know that it has already served its purpose for you. There is no need to feel guilty when you have used the item to the best of your ability. Minimalism will help you master these traits so that they become habits.

You will be amazed to find out just how great living minimally can feel, allowing your home and your mind to be free of clutter and worry.

Introduction

Have you ever felt overwhelmed by the clutter that surrounds you? It becomes a frustrating task to find the things that you need when you are sifting through the items that you have collected over time. The concept of minimalism was introduced to teach you how to live with less. Aside from living with less clutter, you are also ridding yourself of worry over finances and other bothersome stressors. When you assign a space for everything that you own, you are less likely to feel overwhelmed. By practicing minimalism, not only are you going to learn the best techniques to stay organized, but you will also adopt those behaviors into other areas of your life. When you are able to feel satisfied by having the things in life that are necessities, then you are fully encompassing a minimalist lifestyle.

Essentially, you can use minimalism to discover freedom. We have all likely felt weighed down by the responsibility of cleaning our home. When you have many possessions and not enough solutions to store them all, your cleaning process has probably resulted in frustration. This can become a bothersome habit, discouraging you from getting organized again in the future. Minimalism allows you freedom by ridding you of the stress and guilt attached to owning too many material possessions. Nowadays, it is very common for people to participate in consumerism. With all of the latest gadgets and items available that are advertised to make our lives easier, it is natural that we would want to buy these things.

The trick is to unassign meaning from things that are not actually sentimental. You might have a special scrapbook of photographs that depict your family history, and this is understandably an item that you would like to hold onto. Insisting on keeping five sweaters that are nearly identical is not the same thing. If you think about your life on a practical level, you should be able to determine that it is not necessary to own five sweaters that are so similar. You can simplify this by keeping your favorite one. It becomes hard to choose favorites when we make the selection process too personal. At the end of the day, these are sweaters that will either be worn, or end up sitting in your closet. It makes much more sense to keep the one you know you'll wear and donate the others to a good cause.

As you become invested in your minimalist lifestyle, you will see that you develop much more appreciation for the things that you have. There is natural greed within all of us, the desire for more. Teach yourself that you can find satisfaction without making a purchase. In fact, before you make a purpose, minimalism teaches the idea that you can repurpose the items that you already have. This book will guide you through the necessary steps and show you how a minimalist approach to life is possible. People each day are realizing the benefits of minimalism and the happiness that it has the ability to bring forward.

Chapter 1
The Act of Decluttering

"Owning less is better than organizing more." - Joshua Becker

Decluttering is arguably the greatest tool you have in order to achieve a minimalist lifestyle. Most people will need to go through this process more than once to maintain a level of organization that is considered functional. Think of this as a positive step that you are taking toward a more productive life. Do not let yourself dwell on the memories that you have with these items. Instead, focus on the good that they have brought to your life and accept that they have each served a purpose. Sometimes, we obtain items that are only meant to temporarily assist us in some way. It is natural for us to cycle through them. As you become more familiar with it, decluttering can often become therapeutic. It teaches us how to let go without becoming emotionally attached.

Where to Begin

The first thing that you need to do is make an observation about your current living situation. What stresses you out the most to declutter? For some, it is the closet and for others, it is the garage. Consider what aspects are making it hard for you to stay organized. After you think about these things, sit down and make a list of goals that you would like to accomplish. They can be personalized to your own needs, but make sure that you are really aiming to change the things that stress you out the most. A lot of people will go room by room, writing down areas that they would like to declutter. Once you have your home mapped out in this way, assign each area a number between 1 and 10, 1 being the least severe and 10 being in massive need of decluttering.

Use this map as a reference for you to stay on track. Starting with the areas that you have rated the highest, you can begin decluttering. Before you try to organize anything, walk into the space with a trash bag and get rid of items that serve no purpose. There is no point in creating order when there is trash around. You might come across some items that you will no longer use but they do not need to be thrown either; put these into a donate pile. At the end of your decluttering, you can take a trip to your local thrift store and donate these items to people who are actually in need of them.

It helps to set deadlines for yourself. Even though you are decluttering in order to rid yourself of stress, a reasonable timeline can be healthy to follow. Make sure that you are giving yourself realistic deadlines. Consider giving yourself rewards for each deadline that you complete. This makes the task more fun, like a game. It helps to estimate the amount of time that you will need to declutter each area. Cleaning out a closet is probably going to take less time than cleaning out an entire garage. You can base your deadlines off of these estimates that you create. It is possible for decluttering to become a group activity, and this also has the potential to make it more fun. Let other people in the household know what you are doing and when you are doing it.

If you can't see yourself throwing away an item or donating it, you can turn this into a productive solution - hold a garage sale. When you are able to make a small profit off of the items that you are no longer using, you will be able to see the benefits of decluttering. Selling your items assures you they are going to be relocated to people who can find some use for them. Once you get into the momentum of sorting your items, you will see that it can become fun.

Stick to a few general rules as you declutter your home:

- Working Order: Ask yourself if the item still works. As things become outdated, they are also prone to breaking. If you are holding onto a broken item that has no intention of being fixed or utilized in some way, you are holding onto clutter. Make sure that everything in your "keep" pile is actually functional.

- The 80/20 Rule: In general, we use only 20% of the items that we actually own. The other 80% usually are just sitting around and taking up space. This is an especially helpful rule to use while you are trying to declutter your clothing. Consider the last time that you actually wore the item to determine if it is being utilized frequently. The same can be said for other things, considering the last time that you used them for their intended purpose.

- Forget Cost: The price that you originally paid for the item is not going to have much relevance the longer that you hold onto it. This being said, cost should not have much impact on whether or not you keep the item. Factoring in inflation and wear and tear, it is unlikely that you would be able to provide an accurate appraisal of all the items that you own. It always comes down to its functionality. You only need to keep the things that you use regularly and that work.

- **One Night:** If you are having trouble deciding what you want to get rid of, allow yourself to sleep on it for a night. First thing when you wake up the next morning, make your decision. There is nothing wrong with wanting a clear mindset before getting rid of something that you once owned. Discarding things can be tough for some people. Keep the timeframe short in order to prevent procrastination, otherwise you will find yourself stuck in the same cycle of never decluttering your home.

Why It Is Important

Living in a cluttered home can actually begin to take both a physical and an emotional toll on you. Clutter can go beyond an annoyance and transforms into something that causes you to worry on a daily basis. This anxiety is not good for anyone to hold onto. You are already likely stressed out by your job, running the household, and looking after your family. There is no need to add another factor into this already full schedule that you follow. To complete all the required tasks, it is important that you make sure you are taking care of yourself first. If you find that you are making yourself sick from stressing over a cluttered home, this is more reason than ever to begin a minimalist lifestyle.

Only you know exactly how you feel, so the decision to declutter becomes a personal one. The items that you own all become a part of who you are, some for a long time and some only temporarily. While they might be relevant to you, know that some items are only meant to be in your life to serve a specific purpose. Maybe you went through a period where you felt lonely, so you decided to teach yourself how to play the guitar. If your guitar is no longer being used because you have gotten into a relationship and would rather spend time with your significant other, this is an example of something that has served its purpose. While there might be nothing wrong with it and you think you *might* use it again in the future, it is best to get rid of it if you haven't used it in 6 months or more.

When you declutter your items, you are naturally getting rid of some. This is great for when you begin to organize. If you have ever felt frustrated because you cannot find something, it is likely that you would benefit from decluttering. Knowing exactly where something is will save you the time and aggravation from sifting through countless belongings. Decluttering is an efficient solution that is going to put you on the right path toward minimalism. You will learn how to feel content with only holding onto the things that are useful to you. The transition might make you think that you are giving up certain household stuff, but as you settle into the lifestyle, you will realize that you likely won't miss any of the things that you give up. Humans are resilient, and it is natural to regroup and go with the flow when something changes. It isn't easy for everyone, but if you can let yourself transition slowly, you should not have any problems.

Being able to make decisions is a crucial aspect of life. You are going to make thousands of decisions, both big and small. Decluttering allows you to practice this ability. Not only will you get used to choosing which stuff you need to keep, but you will also feel more confident with making other decisions. Holding onto clutter is like giving up on any sense of order. At the moment, you might feel that you have a purpose for keeping everything, but you will come to find out that you aren't truly utilizing each item. The idea behind minimalism is that everything you own should serve a purpose.

Considering your physical health, think about all of the dust and mildew that can build up when you are storing a large number of items. It is likely that you don't get to clean your closet as often as you should. When things stay stagnant in an enclosed space like this, the dust will build up very quickly. Whether you realize it or not, you are breathing in this polluted air on a daily basis. By clearing out your storage spaces, you will notice a difference in the air quality. Breathing will become easier and your allergies become less bothersome.

On a mental level, you might find that you are having difficulty with your concentration. By keeping your physical space cluttered, you are also unknowingly holding onto clutter in your mind. The clarity that you receive when you realize this connection is very powerful. You will find that you are naturally in a calmer state of mind, and tasks that you must accomplish will not feel like such a burden. Overall, you can see that decluttering goes beyond improving your living space. It can lead to an entire lifestyle change.

How to Make It a Habit

Habits that you have been holding onto for years are hard to get rid of. They become ingrained into your muscle memory, and you will probably not even notice when you are acting on them. If you are ready to change your habits, it is going to take a couple of steps. Consider the following as you work on incorporating decluttering into your daily life:

- Make a Commitment: If you can commit to 1-month period of practicing your new habit, then you have a good chance of holding onto it. You must remember that it takes time to condition yourself. Not only are you trying to encourage different behavior, but you also need to unlearn the behavior that you normally act on. There is never a better time to start than right now. Delaying the process won't make it any easier.

- Practice it Daily: Decluttering does not have to involve a huge sweep of your items every single day. While it is great to do this when you are first starting out, it won't really be necessary for the immediate weeks to follow. If you would like to still practice the behavior daily in order to train the habit, you can do so by making sure that you are producing as little waste as possible. This means being considerate about the new items that you bring into your home. Can you store something in a reusable container rather than a single-use box? These little changes are going to get you in the decluttering mindset.

- Utilize Reminders: It can be easy to forget a new habit because it is not yet a part of your regular routine. Use reminders so that you can stay on track. Whether you prefer to write them down or use your phone to help you, reminders are a vital part of holding yourself accountable for your new actions. They can also serve a motivational purpose, as well. Make sure that you check in with yourself at least once a week to ensure that you are still on the right track.

- Work with a Friend: It is likely that you aren't the only person that you know who could benefit from decluttering. Try proposing the idea to your best friend so that you can work on building the habit together. You can even help one another get rid of things. Getting habitual of a new thing becomes easier when you have someone else who can relate to you. This is another way to stay motivated because you will want to maintain the new habit so that you do not let your friend down.

- Create a Trigger: A trigger is something that you can use to encourage yourself to perform your new habit. For example, putting on a playlist of music before you start cleaning will get you into the right mindset. Your trigger can be just about anything you want it to be. Make sure that you keep it lighthearted so that you do not become stressed out before you start. Anything that you choose, it must be something that you do right before you begin decluttering. Your brain will form this association quickly.

- Keep Your Needs Met: While it can be easy to just empty your closet and convince yourself that you have the hang of decluttering, you still need to make sure that all of your needs are met. Just as it does not make sense to hold onto a dozen broken kitchen appliances, it also does not make sense to get rid of the working ones. You still need to be able to cook yourself meals. Practicality is what will prevent you from going too far with your decluttering. If getting rid of something will actually cause you an inconvenience, then you should consider keeping it instead; replacing it is also an option.

- Recognize Imperfection: You aren't going to become an expert overnight. If you complete a month of living your minimalist lifestyle and you still feel that there is more to get rid of, that is okay. What is important is that you have started the processed and formed a habit. Perfection is not what you should be striving for; acknowledge all of the steps that you have taken. The great thing about decluttering is that you can keep going. You are never truly 'done'.

- Get Rid of Temptation: It wouldn't make sense to declutter your home and then go on a shopping spree. This would be counter-productive to all of the progress that you have already made. Being able to deny temptation is going to help you stay organized. While you do not need to cut shopping out of your life entirely, you must make sure that you are also forming smart habits surrounding it. Consider if you actually need to shop or if you are just doing so to fill a void or to kill time.

- Gather Inspiration: As you are forming your habits, it is a great idea to seek inspiration from others. Whether you choose to look at home magazines or model your behavior after a friend who has a knack for organization, this inspiration is going to remind you of what you are working toward. The better you become at decluttering, the more that other people will actually begin to see inspiration in what you are doing.

Chapter 2
Ask Yourself What You Really Need

"You have succeeded in life when all you really want is only what you really need." - Vernon Howard

A big part of living a minimalist lifestyle involves determining what you truly need to live a fulfilling life. It becomes a balance of keeping the things that you need to survive while also including a few extras that are going to make you happy. When you already possess all of the items that you have accumulated, it can be hard to think about living your life without some of them. Considering what you need while you are still in your home environment is probably not going to be very helpful. Take some time to yourself to sit quietly and imagine that you are in an empty room. What are the items that you would require in order to live comfortably? Aside from shelter and a place to sleep, think about the actual items that you would like to have by your side. List them one at a time, carefully considering the value that each item would bring to your life.

Basic Needs

By breaking down your needs in the order of importance, you will realize that the most basic ones revolve around the desire to survive. So, what do you need to survive? Shelter is one thing, and this should already be accounted for within your living space. Normally, there are only a few minor things that need to be done to your actual home in order to declutter. If you have items outside in your yard that could be put away, make sure that you organize them accordingly. Also, be sure to keep your landscaping as clean as you can. A tidy external appearance is going to make you feel great as you walk into your home. This is something that you don't need to spend too much time on because what you actually need already exists within those walls and under that roof.

The next is food and water; luckily, your fridge space is generally not terribly cluttered. You can take a look at the food stock that you have and throw away any expired or unused items. This will make it easier to see what you actually have available to eat. It is also a good idea to go through your cupboards and pantry regularly to do the same thing. Again, this is not something that you need to focus on too much because it is normally not the main source for a person's clutter. It is an essential aspect of survival, though. You will feel great knowing that, from this moment forward, you are no longer going to be wasting any food or drinks. Only purchase items that you know will be consumed.

Sleep is another essentialilty for survival. You need to make sure that your bed is comfortable and clear of clutter before you rest each night. If you have a habit of placing items onto your bed and leaving them there until you can figure out where to put them, nighttime likely becomes stressful. Before you sleep, you should not have to worry about putting things away or moving them so you can lay down. Treat your bed as something that is important for your happiness. This means that you should be respectful, never using it as an additional storage option. When you are able to get straight into bed and relax, you will appreciate your efforts that were made earlier in the day to stay organized.

The air that you breathe within your home is important. Make sure that you check any air filters that you have. Replace them regularly to ensure that the air you breathe is clean. If you have any fans, make sure that you dust them off every week because dust can build up very quickly. If you are using dirty fans, they will simply be spreading polluted air around your home for you to breathe. You will find that the allergies, which you didn't know that you were suffering from, will subside. Life is much more enjoyable when you feel great physically.

Consider if you need to make any home improvements. Your house should protect you from all kinds of weather, hot and cold. If you notice any leaks, cracks, or dents, try to get them taken care of. Understandably, this might have to be fixed on a project basis. Do your best to make a list of anything that must be done so that you can stay on track. You will feel productive knowing that you are aware of what needs to be fixed rather than hoping that nothing is wrong. This knowledge will let you to feel productive and motivated.

Socialization is another necessity for survival; some people need it more than others. When your home is cluttered, it becomes a burden to invite people over. It can also lead you to feel embarrassed or ashamed. By living minimally, not only are you making your own life easier, but you are making it easier to invite others into your space. You should feel proud of your home and confident while hosting other people. Their basic needs are going to be the same as yours. As long as you are taken care of, you will be able to take care of others.

The final element that puts it all together is stability. This will come from settling into your minimalist lifestyle. As you become better at living with less, you will feel that you have a grasp at what must be done. From short-term goals to long-term goals, being able to live free of clutter is going to assist you in accomplishing them all. This is a great way to provide you with security and stability about the life that you are living. It pushes the stress away and encourages you to make practical changes that will help make your life better.

Desires and Goals

Your goals can be anything that you would like to accomplish. Our goals fall into one of two categories: short term or long term. Take a moment to sit down and make a list of all the goals that you can think of. What would you like to get done? These goals don't have to revolve around living minimally. They can be anything that you want. Once you have them all written down on paper, determine which ones can be done within a month and which ones are going to take longer. This will differentiate the short term and long term. Next, place stars next to each one that is meant to be a priority. For example, hiring someone to fix your roof is going to take priority over painting the walls in your room. Use your common sense to see which goals should be dealt with more urgently.

As you make changes to your lifestyle, you should always keep your list of goals handy. Use your goals to make sure that you are staying on the right track. Remember, living minimally does not mean that you need to get rid of everything and stop doing everything. It is about functioning in a more efficient manner with less. Think about ways that you can push your boundaries while still ensuring that your basic needs are being met and your goals are being accomplished. You will find that it takes less than you probably imagined.

Make sure that you update your list of goals on a regular basis. As you complete some, you will probably find that you would like to add more to the list. This is a great habit to fall into because it ensures that you are always thinking ahead. Part of minimalism involves planning for the future. You need to think about your present state of being and also what is coming up. While it is important to only live in the moment, it is smart to prepare yourself for what you are and aren't expecting in the future. You should always aim to have a plan.

Your desires are things that you simply want, mainly material items or possessions that are not physical. Maybe you would like a new car or a romantic relationship. These desires are just as important as your goals because they keep you happy. If you wander through life, hoping that these things will come to you, they might if you are lucky. There is always more that can be done to control the outcome, though. By putting out the type of energy that you would like to attract, you will find that it is easier to get what you desire. This is not a new practice by any means, as even ancient civilizations utilized visualization in order to get what they wanted. Think about what you have done lately in order to secure the things that you desire.

When you have a clear mind, you will be able to focus on these things easily. Worrying about where your items are or how you are going to clean up your messes can impact the way that you feel about yourself. You might feel that you are too worn out at the end of each day to think about anything other than the impending task of cleaning and organization that lies ahead. It becomes a source of stress so powerful that you might not even realize what caused it. This can then devolve into you falling into a bad mood, potentially taking it out on yourself and those around you. As you can see, living in a minimalistic manner can work to improve all of these negative roadblocks that are experienced in life.

When you think about the things that you actually need, know that you are able to survive with the bare minimum, but you do not have to. Minimalism should allow you to feel complete and satisfied. You should never feel that your lifestyle is forcing you to give up the things that enable you to feel comfortable and happy. This is a big misconception about minimalism that keeps people from trying it out for themselves. It is actually a very versatile lifestyle that can transform based on what you need from it. Whether you require less stress or more fun in life, minimalism can help you. Never allow any lifestyle to let you lose sight of your goals and desires.

How to Let Go

You need to realize that being able to let go is the first step to starting a minimalist lifestyle. Even when it is necessary to let go of things, you might find it to be difficult and stressful. This can happen for several reasons but rest assured that you aren't the only one who is going to struggle with this step. As humans, we form an emotional attachment to items fairly quickly. You might have a sweater that you don't like that much but are holding onto it because of a good memory that happened to you while you were wearing it. The goal is to separate the things that are actually emotional and impactful from the physical items that we tend to associate with them. Most of the time, these things exist in your memories. They aren't going anywhere, even despite letting go of their physical associations.

There are some items that we tend to hold onto because they provide us with a sense of security. When life becomes stressful, it is natural to hold onto the things that bring you joy. The thing about this is that they have usually served a temporary purpose. If you have gotten through the tough period in your life successfully, there is no real need to keep the stuff that helped you to feel secure, but you are likely just used to having it around now. A way to justify keeping the item might be that you will need it at a later time. By using this logic, you will keep holding onto things that will only continue to take up space. Learning how to cope with your emotions without holding onto material things is what you must work on. It is the only way that you are going to feel okay about letting go of the things that you use as security blankets.

Fear of being wasteful is another reason why you might have been putting off decluttering. As you prepare to get rid of these material items, know that you can pass them on efficiently. When you declutter, you do not need to throw everything into the trash. As you have read, there are plenty of ways that you can pass your items along to those who will actually have a use for them. If you do not have a loved one that could benefit from the stuff, you can donate it to a thrift store. You will realize how good it feels knowing that certain items that have been sitting on a shelf will now be used regularly.

You need to determine the value of each item that you are holding onto. An easy exercise involves thinking of how much you would pay for the item if you did not already own it. If you come up with an amount that is very low or even zero, then it should be apparent that you do not see much value in the item. This is not a negative thing, however, because this means that you should feel ready to pass the item along. It is a cycle that never has to end. Every new item turns into an old one after some time, so make sure that you are using it to the best of your ability, and then pass it along once you are done. If you get into this habit, you will find that the clutter will naturally disappear.

Procrastination can hinder you as you embark on your new minimalist lifestyle. If you allow your excuses to keep you from decluttering your home, you are probably never going to start unless you find motivational tools. Just because you feel that you cannot tackle all of your clutter at one time, let that idea rest. You do not have to complete everything at once; this is what your goals are for. Even the smallest effort is going to get you one step closer to your minimalist lifestyle. Instead of remaining stagnant because you feel that your efforts aren't going to make a difference, consider the impacts that you could make regardless. Know that it takes steps to complete any major change in life successfully, and minimalism is no exception.

You will begin to gain from letting go. The better you become about being proactive with your decluttering, the more you will learn how to be at peace with the idea of parting ways with some of your items. When you have less, you begin to appreciate the smaller things in life. You are not going to be distracted by quantity and volume any longer. Instead, you will be able to appreciate the way that your belongings help you to live the life that you want to live. As a minimalist, everything that you own should have a distinct purpose. When you are able to get to this point of letting go, you will also feel that you have a more direct purpose as well.

Chapter 3
Learn How to Reuse

"Reuse is the original green collar job." -Mary Ellen Etienne

Reduce, reuse, recycle, this is a phase you should be familiar with. Even though you have heard of the concept before, you might not be sure how to apply it to your own life. Minimalism is going to teach you how to do this. Being able to reuse items that you already own instead of buying new ones is a useful skill to know. Not only does it prevent waste, but it also prevents clutter. Just as you would section off your cleaning duties per room, you can do the same when it comes to thinking about ways that you can reuse items. You can make a list of all the ideas that you come up with that will allow you to live more efficiently.

Benefits of Reusing Items

Those who reuse their items will be the first to tell you how much it can benefit your own life if you are willing to change your habits. Because it can be a big change for most, the task will often seem challenging. It is the same idea that revolves around minimalism--the thought that you are going to have to live in a deprived state. This is a misconception that surrounds reuse. You will come to realize that you can actually feel more fulfilled when you are able to recognize the benefits:

- **Money Saved:** Money is a significant factor in reusing items; you are going to save a lot of it! Naturally, you are going to be buying fewer items as you decide to reuse the ones that you already have. Single-use items appear to have a low price point in general, but if you add up how many times you must purchase them, it just doesn't make any sense. Save your money and find reusable solutions that will work for your household.

- **Emptier Landfills:** When you throw something away, it gets taken to a landfill where it will remain unless it is eventually burned or buried. There are already a few landfills available for all of our waste. If no one is paying attention to their waste levels, these landfills can become too full. When this happens, trash is going to be lining the streets and other livable areas that surround you. Taking the concept of reusing items seriously shows that you are committed to keeping the world a cleaner place. There are unlimited ways that you can do your part, but there is not unlimited landfill space.

- **Less Energy:** When you decide to buy something that is free of packaging, you are saving the fuel of the trucks that would have had to transport all of that raw material to the factory. This consumes a lot more energy than actually transporting the finished product most of the time. Raw materials are bought in bulk, so they are heavier. When there is less consumer-demand for heavily packaged items, companies will have no choice but to create alternative options. Your shopping habits have the ability to show these companies what is in demand.

- Reduced Pollution: More waste is equal to more pollution. Not only is this incredibly harmful to the environment, but it can also impact your health. Those with breathing issues and asthma aren't going to be able to have a good quality of life when the air is filled with toxins. Your quality of life truly depends on your awareness level. Make sure that you are doing your part to preserve the air quality. Plant some trees if you can. Do your best to throw items away that need to be thrown away.

These reasons are backed by science and extensive studies. It is the most logical way to look at the idea of reusing. Aside from the statistics, think about the life that you would like to live. As you aim to live minimally, it just makes sense to begin reusing items. It fits within the most basic principles of minimalism. You aren't going to become better at changing your habits until you immerse yourself in new ones.

Encourage those around you to do the same. While it is not on you to make sure that others are living eco-friendly lives, your voice can make a difference. As people begin to notice the difference that you are making by changing your lifestyle, this might serve as some much-needed inspiration to do the same. It is through these actions that we can all truly make a difference in the state of the world and the quality of life that we are all experiencing.

It is thought that reusing actually benefits the environment more than recycling. While both are great habits to practice, reuse does not involve any additional energy or effort. It is actually one of the most effortless changes that you can make because you already have the items to reuse. Being able to see things from this perspective is going to help you on your journey to minimalism. Before seeking outside items that you must purchase or procure, take a look at the tools that you already have. You will likely find yourself better equipped than you originally thought.

Reuse is going to teach you how to be okay with trial and error. You might create makeshift items out of the things that you already have, only to find that they do not serve their purpose. This is a valiant effort because you tried to make a difference. There is no need to feel discouraged if this happens. Simply try a different solution; the idea is to become a more innovative thinker.

How to Become Savvier

The kitchen is a great place to begin reusing items. There are plenty of things that require storage. Instead of purchasing single-use storage options (like plastic bags), consider switching to glass jars. Mason jars are great for several reasons. They come in a wide variety of sizes, perfect for storing anything. Also, you can put them into the dishwasher to clean when you are ready to reuse them. If you don't feel like stocking up on Mason jars right away, consider which containers you already own that can be reused. Coffee canisters are great for this purpose, sturdy and able to hold many items. Any other glass jar would work as well. When you finish the contents of the jar, you can wash it out and then begin reusing it again.

Cleaning products are important too. You need to use them throughout your home, and you probably purchase them frequently. Instead of buying the same products over and over again, keep an empty bottle and make your own supplies. There are several different recipes that you can follow to make your own natural cleaners with ingredients that you probably already have at home. When you do this, you are able to customize the products to your liking. By incorporating essential oils into the cleaners, you can also customize their smells.

If you have an extra stash of paper around the house, you can use it to make your own envelopes and repurpose it for wrapping paper. Anything else that you don't want to keep can be recycled. The same can be said for old towels. If you can no longer use them for bathing, cut them up and turn them into rags for cleaning. There are many things that you can use these items for other than their intended purposes. If you take the time to think creatively, you might just surprise yourself. The idea of minimalism is to control your needs, so if you are able to rely on a single item to be used in multiple ways, then you are succeeding.

Food can be reused as well, believe it or not. If you don't have one already, you can start a compost pile. Instead of keeping smelly food in your trash can, turn it into a compost that you can use to fertilize your garden. These scraps will be reused in order to help other plants grow. If you ever eat any fruit, consider planting the seeds. When you get into this habit, you will be able to live more self-sufficiently. It is a great feeling knowing that your potential waste is going toward a productive cause.

In the laundry room, you can change your habits to include a more minimalistic approach as well. Reuse your old dryer sheets! There is no reason for you to toss them in the trash after just one use. A dryer sheet can stay fresh for multiple loads of laundry. Once they lose their scent, you can use them for wiping up pet hair. The static cling makes for the perfect way to gather up all of your pet's shedding.

Dryer sheets also work incredibly well when you need to scrub soap scum out of your tub or shower. Its texture makes the soap scum come off in the most effortless way.

Plastic grocery bags are one of the biggest ways that you can remain wasteful. While some states have already banned them, others use them in abundance. It is likely that you already have quite a few in your home. Before you think about getting rid of them for good, consider finding a purpose for the ones that you still have. You can use them as pet waste bags. After you have used them all, make it a point to purchase some reusable shopping bags. These are great, not only for the grocery store but any time that you must shop. Leave them in your car so that you will never forget them when you go shopping.

When you are finished using your toothbrush, save it for cleaning up around your home. A toothbrush has great bristles for getting into those hard to reach places, like in between your tiles. You can turn old toothpaste tubes into funnels, already the perfect shape for assisting you with pouring liquids precisely. All you have to do is cut off the bottom of the tube and clean out the inside of the tip. If you have no use for a funnel, turn it into a piping bag! This trick works great for when you need to frost a cake or cookies. It gives you the precision and control that you need.

Ways to Create Less Waste

When you aim to live waste-free, you are making an even bigger commitment to your minimalist lifestyle. Not only is your input less, but your output will be less too. This is important, especially for lowering your carbon footprint. Without even realizing it, your wasteful habits can be contributing to the destruction of the environment quality. Taking a step toward living waste-free is going to benefit not only your own household but others around you as well. You can become a great example of how to live minimally when you master this step.

As you begin, know that you aren't going to become waste-free overnight, just as you can't become a minimalist overnight. There are steps that you must master and perfect in order to achieve this. By actively practicing the reduce, reuse, recycle mantra, you are putting in an effort toward creating less waste. Think about all of the single-use items that you have in your life right now. Are there any ways that you can eliminate or reuse them? Start here. Most people have a lot of these items around the house, all with a suitable replacement solution.

Stop using paper towels. This is an item that you probably buy frequently, as it is a necessity, or so you thought. Opt for rags instead. You can wipe surfaces with reusable rags that you wash weekly instead of buying rolls of single-use towels. If you have any old sheets that no longer serve a purpose as bedding, you can cut them up into sections to use as napkins. There are many ways that you can banish paper towels for good. As you become better at living waste-free, you will realize that you already have many resources around you. Many items in your home can be modified in order to create less waste.

Packaging is a large source of waste. No matter what you buy, it is likely to come in packaging of some sort. There are ways for you to waste less packing; bringing your own produce bags is one idea. Reusable mesh produce bags make a lot more sense than the plastic ones that are provided at the store. Your fruits and veggies can go straight from the mesh bag into the fridge or fruit bowl. For other items, try to purchase things from companies that support biodegradable packaging. While it might not be possible to get rid of all packaging altogether, it does make a difference when you shop eco-friendly.

You might also be wasting electricity in your house. When you walk out of a room, make a habit of turning off the lights behind you. Not only will you notice a difference in your energy bill, but you will also be preserving a lot of electricity. Living waste-free means thinking outside of the box and being mindful of your actions. Think about the small changes that you can make right now that will make an impact. The same concept applies to water. If possible, cut down on your shower time or even your showers in general. You can save a lot of water by opting for a dry shampoo every other day instead of washing your hair.

If you have a garden, try to invest in some rainwater barrels. Watering your garden can become wasteful if done carelessly or excessively. If you have a certain amount of rainwater that you can use on your garden, you will likely ration it out more efficiently than relying on your water hose. For even more efficiency, bring a small bucket into the shower with you. Allow the bucket to fill as you shower so that you can use the water for your garden or other purposes. You can even use it for cleaning. The point is that you will have an amount of water that was not wasted because you collected it when you were being productive.

When you run your dishwasher or washing machine, make sure that they are full. Instead of running small loads frequently, it makes more sense to just save the water until you have enough to wash a large load. If there is an energy-efficient mode, make sure that you are utilizing it. You will find that your routine becomes more succinct when you operate this way. Each action is going to serve a purpose that you can feel great about. Knowing that you are reducing your own waste is something to be proud of. It is a step toward a healthier environment and a minimalist lifestyle.

Chapter 4
Quality Over Quantity

"Truth is ever to be found in the simplicity, and not in the multiplicity and confusion of things." -Isaac Newton

Consumerism revolves around the concept of *more*--we are taught to buy, see, and do more. While it is important to have enough food, shelter, and items to meet your basic needs, the rest can be reduced. Have you ever purchased something that you did not need simply because it was on sale? This is how companies try to push their products on consumers, creating a need for something when there truly might not be one. It is essential to consider this when you are out shopping. Are you simply buying things because you can or because you need them? Minimalism will teach you that quality is far more important than quantity. You will learn how to be happy with the things that you have while accepting that you do not need to purchase something just because it is being suggested to you.

Why a Splurge Pays Off

As you buy the items that you have determined that you need, it is still possible to put a minimalist spin on the process. Spending money does not sound like it would be one of the steps toward minimalism, but think about the bigger picture, the more that you spend upfront on quality items, the less you will have to spend in the future to replace them. Making a splurge can be warranted if you know that it is going to last you for a long time. Think about the frequency at which you must replace your roof. You wouldn't want to opt for cheap materials because this would result in a roof replacement every 5 years. By selecting quality materials, you can go 20-30 years with the same roof. Thinking about your own life in these terms is going to help you determine when it is an appropriate time to spend a little bit of extra money.

Despite any debt that you are currently in, there are still some things that are worth splurging on. Buying these things can actually assist you in paying off your debt without needing to worry about additional expenses that might come up. The first is healthy food. Without your healthy physical body, you would be unable to function. Your work must be put on hold, and all of the household tasks that you maintain will be left unless someone else can take them on. A lot of people underestimate their health because they do not see it as a priority. When you eat healthily, you are putting yourself first. This is necessary for so many aspects of life, and it is not worth the risk of falling ill. By spending the extra money on nutritious foods, you can skip out on the doctor's visit that you would likely end up needing.

Your safety is another vital thing to splurge on. This can be taken in several different ways. Consider this example - your car is running fine, but the check engine light keeps coming on. Because you do not want to spend any money, you ignore this for months until your car finally breaks down on the side of the highway. Now, not only do you need to fix your car, but you need a tow truck and a ride home. If you had simply taken care of your car in the beginning, you would have avoided the hassle and the danger of being stuck on the side of the road. Anything that impacts your safety in any way is a worthwhile splurge. You don't even need to think about it as a splurge because safety is important. Pay attention to the things in your life that you have been putting off. Take care of the ones that can potentially put you or your family in danger.

A working phone is a luxury, but it can also be a useful tool. Having a phone that serves multiple purposes is worth a splurge. Whether you have a decent phone right now or are holding off because you refuse to splurge, you might want to reconsider. Aside from keeping you in contact with your loved ones, your phone can actually assist you with your minimalist lifestyle. To start, any paper and pens are instantly replaced by the notepad and calendar on your phone. Keep track of your schedule and your goals this way. There are also unlimited apps that can help you, keep you entertained, and more. Browse the app store for apps that you might find helpful. Whether the app is meant to help you organize or give you motivation each day, if it is useful, then download it. There are too many things that you can do with a smartphone that makes it a worthy item to spend money on. Plus, if you have a decent phone that you take care of, you will be less likely to purchase one again next year. Try to keep it in the best condition that you can.

Make sure that you have a wardrobe for every occasion. This does not mean that you need to go out on a shopping spree, but you must be prepared for any season and any event that you find yourself a part of. Consider if you have clothing to wear for a professional event, like a work meeting or presentation. You also need to keep in mind that you must have appropriate options for a wedding or a birthday celebration. Aside from the events, make sure that you also have clothing that you feel comfortable in. You need to be able to put on a comfortable outfit and relax while you are at home. Clothing is one of the first things that you might be tempted to give away and donate in order to keep your belongings clean and organized. While it makes sense to get rid of the items that you do not wear, hold onto the things that can serve multiple purposes. For example, a blazer might be formal enough for a special event yet dressy enough for a night out. Consider which of your clothing items are able to do the same thing.

Investing in Your Future

Any time that you must spend a larger amount of money upfront, think about it as an investment toward your future. You might go ahead and buy a crib, stroller, car seat, and highchair as a splurge. These items are going to be used by your family for years to come; it is an investment. If you are ever feeling unsure about making a purchase, consider if it is something that is only going to serve you temporarily or if it will last longer. Things like spa treatments and cups of coffee aren't going to serve you in the future. These are temporary fixes that, while being incredibly beneficial in the moment, serve no purpose to you once they are gone. Prioritization becomes key when you are determining if a purchase is worthy of your hard-earned money.

As a minimalist, you must become aware of determining value. While you might be able to see the value in something like a sports car, consider what this will actually mean for your own life. Will it bring you happiness? Yes. Is it a practical solution for a family that hopes to have children one day? Probably not. When you consider your future, it is best to do so in several different ways. There is the immediate future which stems from weeks to months, the near future which can be months to a year, and then the far future, which means that you need to be thinking longterm. While you are determining if something is truly worth buying, ask yourself if the item is going to benefit you in all of these ways. If you can't think of any significant reason, then you might need to hold off on making the purchase.

As you begin to live minimally, ask yourself regularly if all of the items in your possession are serving their purposes. You might own things that are working for you right now but could be improved to function more efficiently. Allow yourself to let go of the things that will no longer serve you in the future. Know that it is much easier to begin this process now while there is time rather than scrambling to get rid of or update items at the moment. Being a minimalist means that you are always one step ahead. You should never feel that you don't have any options or don't know what to do. Preparedness becomes one of your main traits as you live minimally.

When you put a value on every item that is not monetary-related, you begin to see which things you actually need and what you simply want. Your desires are valid, as we have discussed, but the way that you prioritize them is what becomes important. There might be hundreds of things that you want and that will make you happy, but that does not mean that you are going to go out and buy them all in one day. Moderation is necessary if you would like to keep up a minimalist lifestyle. You will come to find that holding off on purchasing an item that is only a temporary want can change your mind. You might realize that you don't actually want the item anymore after all because it is no longer relevant to you. These are great realizations. They might lead you to desire new things that are actually going to benefit you.

Rid yourself of the guilt that you feel when you decide to make a purchase. You might be living fearfully at this moment because of all the clutter this has led you to. Know that it is possible to invest in your future while simultaneously sorting through the belongings that you already have. Seeing everything in front of you is going to give you insight into what you have in abundance and what you lack. Don't be fearful that you are going to be stuck in the cycle of clutter forever. Minimalism teaches you many tips and tricks that you can utilize through every stage of your life. Whether you are a single individual living in the household or one member of an entire family, you will find that minimalism can help you keep track of what you actually need in order to have the most fulfilling life possible.

Avoiding Tempting Deals

In our current culture, saving money is a huge tactic that is being pushed in order to convince you to make a purchase. Whether you are driving down the road and seeing billboards or skimming through your favorite clothing website, it is possible that you are going to see deals advertised to you left and right. They draw us in because they promise savings. This makes a purchase sound like a great idea, something that can save you money. What a lot of people fail to realize is that they never needed to spend the money in the first place. You have probably been impacted by a buy-one-get-one type of sale at some point in your life. While you are browsing a store, you might have felt the need to purchase the item and then you ended up leaving with two. This is a pretty great deal, but did you even need either of the items in the first place?

It is crucial that you make the distinction between the things you really need and the things that are being advertised to you. Deals are always going to exist, and they can often convince you to spend your money when you really shouldn't. How will you be able to say no to certain offers when they are constantly being pushed on you? Minimalism is going to teach you about which items are necessary for survival and daily living. When you see a seemingly great offer, consider if it fits into your new lifestyle. Is there an immediate, useful purpose that you can assign to the item without it taking up storage space and sitting there for an extended time? Another way that you might convince yourself to buy something is the thought that you *might* be able to use it at a later date. In minimalism, there is no maybe. Each item that you own should serve a clear purpose.

Being able to acknowledge the value and necessity of any deal is also important. While the deals might sound great, consider if you need to be spending money in the first place. Imagine that you see a 50% off sale on a BBQ grill. Unmistakably, you are going to see this as a great deal. If it is a $200 grill, you'd be able to get it for $100. If you have a perfectly working BBQ grill at home, spending that $100 would not make any sense while you are trying to follow a minimalist lifestyle. That money would be an unnecessary expense that would lead you to clutter. You would either need to get rid of your other grill or keep both. Minimalism teaches you to hold onto what you already have until you no longer have a purpose for it. Because you can acknowledge that you do not need to buy a new grill at the moment, this means that you still value the one that you already have.

The same philosophy applies to smaller deals, too. It can become fairly easy to train yourself to avoid deals on the same scale as the one above, but the smaller ones can become a challenge. When you are checking out at the grocery store, it is likely that you have browsed through the gum and magazines even though you didn't need either. Sometimes, these items are put on sale for a fairly cheap price. This makes sense if you went to the store for either item; it would be a justified purpose if that were the case. However, if you simply get a magazine just "because it's a dollar," then you have just given in to that consumerist mentality that minimalism tries to correct. Much like the prior example, it makes sense to get a magazine only if it would serve a direct purpose in your life.

As you are training yourself to see these deals for what they actually are, know that you are not missing out on anything. The urgency that is placed behind advertising is what normally pushes you to make purchases that are unnecessary or unimportant. They convince you that the deals are temporary and that you need to take immediate action. Before you fall victim to this tactic again, truly consider what you would be able to accomplish if you were to purchase the item. The switch to a minimalist lifestyle is all about a change of perception.

Chapter 5
Keep What Makes You Happy

"If you aren't grateful for what you already have, what makes you think you would be happy with more?" -Roy T. Bennett

Minimalism isn't all about getting rid of the things that you love. It encourages you to keep what makes you happy because this is a valid reason to keep something in itself. Normally, this includes things that have sentimental value behind them. Hold onto photos, items that were passed down to you by loved ones, and gifts that you treasure. The decision is going to be personal but know that you do not need to feel like you must let go of the items that mean the most to you. What must be done after you determine which items you are keeping, is to make sure that they all have their own designated space or purpose.

There are ways that you can honor your favorite things without allowing them to become forgotten on a storage shelf. From shadow boxes to put your belongings on display to locations that allow the items to be seen, you can repurpose your favorite things in order to make them more useful in your life. Living minimally does not mean to live miserably. Get rid of the notion that you must go without the things that mean the most to you. This is a common reason that people do not choose to partake in a minimalist lifestyle; they believe that you must get rid of everything, no questions asked. There is actually a sense of flexibility with minimalism. You are able to control what you keep and how you use the items that you own.

Items That Hold Memories

Sometimes, you might want to hold onto an item that is merely associated with a memory. For example, the object might be a particular bottle of perfume that you were using when you first met your significant other. Keeping that for any other reason would seem wasteful and useless, but it becomes meaningful when it has personal meaning behind it. You can turn that empty perfume bottle into a beautiful vase or a way to display a candle. The things that you hold onto don't simply just need to sit in storage. It is likely that you will see the item and appreciate it more when you decide that you'd like to repurpose it. Think about all of the sentimental belongings that you currently own. How many of them are being repurposed?

This action has become known as sentimental upcycling. It is an idea that you can pair with minimalism to ensure that you are being as smart as possible about the things that you hold onto. Fabric is something that is often kept because of the memories associated with it. It is common to have a couple of old pieces of clothing that you no longer wear because they don't fit your personal style now, yet you enjoy reminiscing about the event(s) that happened while wearing them. If you know that you are not going to be wearing something again, consider utilizing the fabric for a different purpose. Quilting is a great tribute to clothing that is important and memorable to you. You can keep all of that you hold dear while saving only small pieces of it. The quilt that you create will feel entirely personal and each square is going to remind you of the memory that you have been holding onto.

Oversized clothing, which was passed down to you from a loved one, can also be repurposed. Instead of letting your grandfather's shirts remain unused in the back of your closet, consider turning them into messenger bags. It is a fairly easy project, and it allows you to get some use out of the item instead of letting it sit around. You can also turn these unused clothing items into the fabric for doll clothing or stuffed animal clothing. If you have children, this can become an enjoyable and meaningful project to take on that allows you to use the fabric for a better purpose.

Frame your photos. Instead of keeping them stored inside of a photo album that is collecting dust on your shelf, try framing the ones that mean the most to you. This is a way to ensure that you are appreciating your photos while also creating wonderful decor items to fill your space. Having these photos on display will remind you of the moments that you love, therefore boosting your mood. Happiness is an important aspect of minimalism. If you feel that the lifestyle is making you unhappy, then you are doing something wrong. Always know that you are able to include the things that make you happy in minimalism. There is never going to be a time where you should feel forced to get rid of these personal belongings.

Chances are, you might have a collection of dishware that is taking up a lot of space inside of your cupboards. If you have any broken items from the collection, you can upcycle them by turning them into pendants. Placing each cracked piece inside of a small frame that can allow you to wear it as a necklace is a great solution to all of the broken sentimental dishware that you might be holding onto. It is a way to honor your family heirlooms without feeling bad about keeping them stored up for extended period of time. Broken plates can also be turned into earrings, bracelets, and rings too. Your creativity is going to become helpful to you in this situation. Allow yourself to think outside of the box.

Consider passing down some of the sentimental items that you own to other members of your family or others who would find meaning in them. Sometimes, sentimental items are only meant to be kept for a temporary period of time until they are passed on. Consider gifting some of the items that you have to your children or siblings. This is a way to cut down on the amount of stuff that you keep while still remaining confident that the items are going to be in good hands. Things that are relevant to an entire family can almost always be passed on for generations. Know that when you let go of these items, you are not simply throwing them away. They are going to be serving a different purpose by being kept by another member of the family. Your time with these items is something that cannot be taken away from you and that you can cherish.

How to Feel Satisfied with What You Have

Counting your blessings is an important process. It is a way for you to check-in with yourself and with your life. By what you are thankful for, you can probably learn a lot about what you value most. For many people, family and friends mean a lot. Jobs are also normally on this list of gratitude. Pets might even make an appearance. So far, these things aren't even material items. No matter what is going on in your life, your list of blessings is one that will remind you of all the good things that you have, figuratively speaking. The process does not stop here. You can actively count your blessings as you live your life. When you eat your breakfast, be thankful that you have breakfast to eat. As you cut the grass in your front yard, be thankful for the abundance of grass. Changing your perspective changes your attitude.

In a culture where more equates to better, you might be confused or misled, thinking that you do not have enough to keep you satisfied. It is easy to become almost addicted to this need for more. Much like any other addiction, you might not even realize that you are doing this. As discussed, it is perfectly normal to want and desire things, but that does not mean that what you already have should go unappreciated. When this pattern begins, no matter how much you have, you will never fully appreciate it. Try counting your blessings without the mention of any physical items at all. If it is hard to do this, then you might need to reevaluate what is truly important to you and why.

Minimalism is going to change the way that you see your life, making way for more appreciation and gratitude. Not only is it a way of life, but it is also a mentality. When insecurities creep in, it normally indicates some level of inferiority. Minimalism can humble you and allow you to see that you do not need to possess the same qualities or items that most others have in order to live a happy life. It is about being happy with what you have right now and being thankful that you have anything at all. Volunteer work is recommended. Doing good deeds can be an eye-opening experience, showcasing just how trivial material items can be. If you are struggling with finding your own gratitude, see if you can experience someone else's.

Being able to feel the joy that other people are feeling is a very empathic approach. It helps to ground you and truly allows you to connect with the world. The more that you practice this type of empathy, the easier it will be to become appreciative of your own situation. Another thing to remember is that nothing stays the same forever. Think about your last five unhappy times. It is likely that they have been resolved or you have moved on from them. Even when things seem like they will not change, it is inevitable that they will. What you get to decide is if you'd like them to change for the better or for worse. This is why maintaining a level of gratitude is important. Your attitude toward life has the ability to shape what happens to you.

Think about all of the times when you wished you had something, worked hard to obtain it, and then received it. There is nothing lucky or unlucky enough to stop you from living the life that you hope for. What matters most is how you treat yourself, your belongings, and those around you. Think about your household like a sanctuary. You come home from work or running errands to feel welcomed and relaxed in your home. This should be a safe place for you to retreat from the world, or to simply just settle down until you are moving onto the next task. When you are thankful for everything that you have inside of your home, it makes the space even more of a sanctuary. Everything will have meaning, and you will be able to feel happy and confident in your decision to keep each item. When there is too much clutter, your possessions tend to lose meaning. Instead, you might come home and get stressed out by thinking about where you are going to store all of your items. Turn this into a peaceful experience; be thankful for what you do keep around your living space.

Ways to Bring Meaning to Your Home

For some, there is a lack of meaning inside of the home. This could indicate that you do not have a connection with the items that you have. If your house feels anything less than a safe space that you feel comfortable spending large amounts of time in, you might need a simple change of scenery. A dirty house becomes a stressful house very easily. When you have too many chores to accomplish than you have time for, being at home is like being at a second job. While you might try your best to relax and ignore the clutter, it has a way of impacting you, even on a subconscious level. When this happens, you might even begin to form some resentment about being at home or not having a nice home. This can often lead you down a path of negativity and selfishness. In order to avoid this, you do not need to do a marathon of cleaning in order to feel at home in your own home. What you must do is bring more meaning inside.

Gaining meaning does not necessarily equate to gaining any physical items at all. In fact, on your search for a meaningful environment, you might find that it actually makes more sense to get rid of things. When you pick up a bag of trash, you don't wish that the trash would stay in your home longer, right? These same feelings can apply to things that simply no longer resonate with you. One example, a work uniform from years ago; Maybe you loved that job, but you have moved on already. Now, the uniform takes up space in your closet and you don't know what to do with it. You probably aren't going to wear it, so get rid of it. Hold onto the things that make you feel your best.

For things that you are going to keep because they are necessities, modify them so that they have meaning. You can place a drawing that your child made onto the fridge to make the fridge something that you enjoy looking at. Little steps like this make a huge difference in the quality of your environment. While you don't need to go around decorating your whole home in personal items, a few of them throughout might be enough to do the trick. Your home is your own space to do what you wish with; it is a lot of freedom of choice. There are very few instances where you will have this much control over the direction of the space. Use this to your advantage by making it feel the best that you can.

Make sure that you are honoring your favorite items while letting go of the ones that no longer have meaning. If you live in a household with other people, get some input on what they find meaningful. Their answers just might surprise you. People are so unique and different from one another; what one finds valuable, another might see as useless. Nothing is set in stone. Even things that were once very meaningful to you can eventually serve their purpose. This does not necessarily take away from their meaning, but it does show your maturity in being able to acknowledge that the item no longer serves you and your life.

Think about minimalism as a ground-up approach. Starting from the very root of your being, this is where you value things that are necessary for survival. As we have talked about these things, you should know which of your possessions falls into this category already. The base of the tree should be made up of things that you do not need, but that you choose to keep because of the purpose that they serve. As the tree branches out, this is where your needs and desires fall. Each branch has the ability to either thrive and grow or become dried out and rotten. Make sure that you keep your tree healthy by feeding it a balance of what you actually need and some of the things that you want. Giving in to your desires too much equates to overwatering the tree. You need to make sure that you are being reasonable.

Chapter 6
How to Purge

"Clear clutter - make space for you." -Magdelena Vandenberg

The act of purging when it pertains to minimalism is actually a fairly therapeutic one. As the day approaches when you are going to do your first cleaning purge, make sure that you begin with a clear mind. Starting with a mindset that is already unwilling to believe in the process will only lead to resentment. Begin once you truly feel that you are ready to let go of things. Remember, a purge is healthy. When you are no longer burdened by the items that you have been holding onto for these months or years, you will feel like a weight has been lifted off your shoulders. Instead of worrying about cleaning or where to put things, you can shift your focus on obtaining things in life that provide you with new meaning. Your goals will feel more attainable, and your spirits will be lifted.

Purging does not mean that you must get rid of all the items you currently own to start from scratch. It actually encourages the opposite. You should hold onto the things that you can find uses for. As you purge, you might discover things that have been put up in storage that were simply forgotten about. This is your chance to decide what you would actually like to keep in your home. Remember, make sure that each item you keep has a purpose for you. Whether it is a sentimental item or an item that is going to be used on a regular basis, you will want to ensure that it has a purpose.

Meaningless items that have already served their purposes tend to get put back up in storage or forgotten about after some time.

When you plan out how you are going to purge, the process is fairly similar to the decluttering one. The difference here is that you are not going to be organizing the items or making them more efficient. You essentially have two choices: keep or discard. Make it simple on yourself; don't think too hard about each item. If you go with your first instinct, you are usually making the right decision. You shouldn't have to spend more than five minutes on each item in order to determine if it is useful or not in your current stage of life. If you do choose to discard something, remember that you do not have to throw it away. You can donate it or pass it on to someone who will get more use out of it. Purging your items is a lifestyle upgrade, one that will make your life more enjoyable. Allow yourself to get rid of the things that stress you out.

Parting with Things You No Longer Need

In order to define what is no longer needed in your life, you must make an observation of where you currently stand. Are you living alone, or do you have a family? Are you career-oriented? Do you enjoy traveling? Knowing yourself well is important for this step. Observe what you enjoy doing while you are at home. Some people use their homes as sanctuaries, places to decompress and unwind. Others love to entertain guests and hold gatherings. No matter what you prefer, know that your purging needs to mirror your actions. It wouldn't make sense to keep copious amounts of kitchen cutlery unless you host people regularly. Just as it wouldn't make sense to keep a bunch of camping gear if you prefer to relax indoors. Use your common sense to justify what you will be keeping.

Your process is going to be unique in the way that you might need less or more time than the average person to purge your items. On average, this process is normally done over 1-2 weekends. If you feel that you can get it done in one day, great! If you feel that you need a month, that is also okay. What matters is that you are starting the process. Even if you prepare yourself to purge, it can still be a bit overwhelming if you have never done it before. You are going to have to look through the items that you probably haven't even picked up in a year. This is important, though. Not only are you taking note of what you currently have, but you will also be able to accept the fact that it is time to let go. It might sound funny but letting go of material items can be an emotional process. These are the items that you have owned for some time, so it is natural that they have become a part of you in some way.

Think about all of the time and effort that will be saved when you need to find something after you purge. Naturally, since you will have less, you won't have to sift through other things to get to what you need. Also, the items that you do end up keeping will all have designated purposes and spaces for storage. There will be no more running late but being unable to leave because you can't find your keys. Minimalism is going to make your life run like a well-oiled machine. As long as you can keep up with the maintenance, then you will be able to follow this lifestyle for the long run. Nobody can force you to live minimally, but when you do make the decision for yourself, you will be glad that you did.

Work on your purge for 30 minutes at a time, taking breaks in between. Sometimes, it can be beneficial to just step outside for a moment in order to clear your head. The process can become mechanical, and that is draining. If you feel that you are taking too long to decide what to keep and what to get rid of, this might signify that you need to take a short break. Make sure that you don't step away for too long because then you might lose momentum in your progress. Take a couple of minutes to breathe in a different space, and then go back in and try again. Your intuition should be flowing during this process, for this is what will guide you to your final decisions. Try to listen to that very first thought that pops into your head when you pick up an item. Make sure that you have distinct piles for the items so that you know what you intend to keep and what you intend to get rid of.

The act of staying organized while you purge is like a precursor to your new lifestyle. In order to stay organized, you need to make things as clear for yourself as possible. Have a trash bag ready to throw away the things that are able to just be discarded. In a separate pile, you should be putting donations and hand-me-downs there. On a table or on the floor, you can put all of the items that you intend on keeping for yourself. When you are able to do this room-by-room, you will see how the system allows you to stay organized. Plus, once all the items are sorted, this gives you a chance to go in and clean all of the surfaces that you normally do not have access to.

Getting Rid of Guilt

It is a common occurrence to feel guilt after you have let go of your items. This comes naturally with purging, and it is something that you need to develop a tougher skin for. Being a little bit sad after you purge is healthy because it shows that you had to make some significant choices. This sadness and guilt should not linger, though. Instead of focusing on what you no longer have, you should be looking toward the future. Think about how efficient your life is going to be now that you are not burdened by clutter. Your items are going to be cleaned and organized, and you won't have to worry about not being able to find things when you need them most. Know that you did the purge because you wanted to give yourself a better life. Minimalism teaches you how to be happy with the things you have, no matter how much you have or how long you have had them.

The things that you purged were not being used fairly. They were either forgotten about in storage or being hoarded for future use. Maybe they were duplicate items of the things that you already have that work. Either way, you get rid of these things because you didn't have a purpose for them. As your items move on to their next chapter, they are actually going to be utilized as intended. Whether you have donated some clothing to a thrift store or passed down some appliances to your little sister, the items were moved because they can find new purposes elsewhere. You should feel proud of yourself for making the accomplishment of coming to a final decision. It can be incredibly difficult to commit to purging, but once you do it, you are so close to living the minimalist lifestyle that you desire.

Regarding what you had to throw away, know that you could not have utilized these items, nor could anyone else. It doesn't make any sense to keep something around that can serve no purpose whatsoever, just for the sake of easing your guilt. Think back on your list of necessities and desires, these are the things that should matter to you. When something cannot even be repurposed, you should know that it is okay to let go of it. Otherwise, it is just going to burden you by taking up space and stressing you out. You do not need to put this kind of pressure on yourself. Be thankful for the purpose that it served in your life and move on.

Having a clear sense of your goals is going to help you avoid guilt. The feeling of guilt usually comes from an action that you do not fully support. Maybe you act out of character, and this will lead you to feeling guilty. If you are committed to purging, know that it is an intentional act. You are making this choice, and you are doing so for a better lifestyle. Again, a bit of sadness is a normal feeling after you have purged, but that is as far as you should take the negativity. Allow yourself to feel it, accept it, and then keep moving forward. Minimalism only begins with the purge. You still have a lot of other decisions to make and work to put in.

Think about how peaceful you will feel when you are in your clean home. Your thoughts will no longer be occupied by messes that you have to clean and storage that you have to organize. Everything that you need will be exactly where you put it, exactly as intended. It is a very freeing feeling that minimalism gives you. It teaches you how to be okay with letting go, and that is a trait that not everybody possesses. You can learn it if you are willing, though. Allow yourself to purge and think about these positive aspects that are just around the corner for you.

Make Purging a Regular Occurrence

When you first start out in minimalism, the initial purge that you tackle is likely going to be your largest one. This makes sense because you are just starting from the beginning. You will have a lot of items that you have probably been holding onto for quite some time. Know that after you accomplish this purge, any future purging is going to be much easier. When you have fewer items, it is going to become harder to let them build up to what they were before you started living minimally. This is why it is important to make sure that you have plenty of energy for your first purge. It is going to be a day or two of work, but you will feel so grateful that you followed through with the process.

You might be wondering how often you should purge after this. The answer truly depends on your habits and upkeep. If you start off strong and maintain your minimalism very well, you might not have to purge again for another year. No one is perfect, though. It can be very easy to fall off the bandwagon, and that is understandable. After your first purge, check-in with yourself after three months. Assess the cleanliness of your home and your ability to find exactly what you need inside of it. If things are still looking good, check back again in another three months. This is a pretty standard habit to get yourself into. You might not always need to re-purge, but it is better to double-check than let the clutter build up again.

After a holiday is a time when you are likely to obtain a bunch of new items. Gift-giving season is one where people find that they usually begin hoarding again. It can be difficult to judge gifts that were given to you but remember that you are doing this for the item's greater purpose. If you have been given something that you know you aren't ever going to use, see what you can do to move it along to a situation where it will be utilized. Even when items aren't purchased by you, they must go through the same assessment. Consider what purpose they will serve in your life. Is it temporary or more long term? Know that it is okay to decide this for yourself.

When you get into the habit of doing anything, it becomes much easier. You will find that you can actually feel enjoyment from purging your items. If you are expecting it, then it is less likely that you will form a stressful association with it. Know that you are in control of the entire experience. What happens during your purge revolves around your actions and your methods. If you find that something isn't working as well as it should be, you have the ability to change it until it feels right. Not every purge is going to be the same. You might need to take more breaks on certain days, depending on what items you are sorting through. Other times, you might feel that purging is incredibly easy. Listen to yourself and make adjustments as needed.

A purge doesn't always need to be a whole-house event. The act of purging can be done on a much smaller scale. If you notice that your house seems clean, but your kitchen drawers are in need of some work, focus on purging them. You can open each drawer and go through the steps of purging without actually needing to dismantle your entire living space. These mini purges will help prevent you from needing to do larger ones like the first one that you accomplished. This gets you into the habit of becoming a resourceful and tidy individual. You gain a sense of accomplishment from all of the purging that you do, and you should feel proud of yourself because it shows that you are making a commitment to a better lifestyle.

Chapter 7
Replace Items You Already Own

"You can't reach for anything new if your hands are full of yesterday's junk." -Louise Smith

Item-replacement is a big part of the minimalist state of mind. If you take a look at your items after you have purged what is no longer necessary, you will see a basic foundation-level of things that you feel are necessary to maintain a fulfilling lifestyle. This isn't to say that the items you see before you are the only items that you will continue living with. There are options for replacement as certain things become susceptible to wear and tear. You might find that you only need to replace parts of certain things in order to keep them functional and useful. You will also learn how to apply your knowledge of minimalism as you purchase new items, successfully avoiding any mass marketing that is geared toward purchasing things that you do not truly need.

Self-control is the main skill that you will be exercising during this step. Once you get here, you should already know that you have enough self-control to part with some of your items that have been deemed no longer useful. This should give you the motivation to take your minimalism one step further toward even more functionality and efficiency. Replacing your items can be similar to upgrading them in some ways. While you won't always obtain a newer or better version of something, the one that you do select should serve a purpose that is greater than the one you already have. This is a great general rule to stick with while you decide what needs to be replaced and what should be left alone.

How to Excel at Replacement

Assess all of the items that you are left with and consider how well each of them works to serve their purpose. You might have an alarm clock that works decently, but the batteries die very quickly in it. This would be an example of an already-functional item that seems to be in need of a replacement. Getting a better alarm clock serves a greater purpose by reliably waking you up and working more consistently. With each item that you are considering replacing, you just have to do this simple assessment to confirm if it is worth changing. The replacement does not have to happen like purging because the items that you decided to keep are ones that already serve a functional purpose. You can take a slower approach in terms of when you would like to replace each item.

Money should be taken into consideration when you are going to be replacing several items. Spending a lot of money all at once to replace things that already function does not follow the guidelines of minimalism. Instead, save your money until you know that you have enough to cover the expenses. Make it a goal to replace your items, one per week or month, depending on how many you would like to replace. This does not have to be a time-consuming process because you already have items that are functional, so this removes a lot of the stress from the process.

Aside from the material items that you own, certain household items will inevitably need to be replaced as well. While this is not a need for concern, you should make sure that you are keeping track of anything that appears worn out or functions at a lower capacity from what it used to. Some examples of these items can be found below:

- Alarms and Extinguishers: Your smoke alarms, carbon monoxide detectors, and fire extinguishers all must be replaced regularly. In some cases, only the battery needs to be changed. But in others, you will need to have a professional come to your home in order to certify that it is in working order. These things are often forgotten about because they are not frequently used, though they are working 24/7.

- Water Filters: Anything that relies on a water filter, such as your refrigerator, coffee machine, or portable water pitcher, must be replaced on a regular basis. When you don't replace these filters, the water is not being purified as it should be. Not only is this an inconvenience, but it can also lead to some health risks if not taken care of.

- Toothbrushes: It is said that in order to remain sanitary, you should replace your toothbrush every 3-4 months. A lot of time can pass while using the same toothbrush without even thinking about it. In this time, a lot of bacteria has the ability to build up. Instead of cleaning your mouth, you will simply be ingesting these bacteria. This is especially true if you get sick. Replace your toothbrush right after you get over any colds or flu viruses.

- Pillows: A lot of gems get absorbed into your pillows, even despite being covered in pillowcases. You should be replacing them every 1-3 years in order to keep them fresh. You can also wash them in between uses. Placing your pillows in the washing machine can be a great way to thoroughly clean them when spot cleaning isn't enough. By doing both of these things, you shouldn't need to replace them as frequently.

By staying on top of replacing these items regularly, you will be able to maintain an efficient routine. Minimalism encourages you to maintain a natural flow in the way that you are living. When you are prepared, you will feel less burdened by the simple task of replacement. Stress tends to build up when you allow yourself to run out of items or to use up items. By eliminating this factor, you will find a natural calmness in your ability to continue focusing on the things that require more of your attention. This type of distribution is what allows for you to maintain a lifestyle that works for you, rather than one that you must work for.

Treating Yourself to New Items

There will come a time when you must buy new items in order to function at your best. You can apply the same principles of feeling productive when buying new items that you need as you do when you are getting rid of the things you do not need. Remember, minimalism isn't only about living with less. The other side of it allows you to obtain new things that will actually help you become even more productive and efficient. The trick is to learn how to differentiate between which items are necessary to purchase and which items you think you must purchase. This concept goes hand-in-hand with some of the methods that have already been discussed. It is important to master this habit because it will set you up with a strong foundation.

When you determine that you must buy something new, know that you deserve it. No matter what the item is, you have come to this conclusion by using a careful thought process. You deserve to have all of the things that you need in order to live a fulfilling life. For example, if you enjoy sewing, getting a new batch of patterns is going to benefit your life. It will fuel your hobby while also encouraging you to make garments. Getting something new also naturally provides you with a boost of positive feelings. Allow yourself to feel good about treating yourself.

Balance is important in any lifestyle. Minimalism teaches you that you should not obtain something new just because you are sad or feeling low. Buying something new should revolve around functionality. Because making a purchase does give you control over your life, you need to be aware of this. A lot of people become cluttered with items that they do not need simply because they enjoy this feeling of control that purchasing provides. While it is a natural human instinct to want control over what is happening in life, there are other ways to get it. Just as there are other ways to boost your mood when you are feeling down. Minimalism forces you to think about the differences in these things, opening your mind to your current habits.

People find that embracing minimalist concepts actually helps boost their happiness more than frivolous shopping does. You might not realize it at first, but the more that you apply these guidelines to your own life, you will see how great it can feel to only spend money toward items that are going to improve your life over time. Temporary and instant gratification is a huge crutch that a lot of people hold onto in order to maintain control. While it can seem like a good idea at first, it does not last, and you will end up feeling the way that you were initially. As soon as you are able to see this difference, you are going to have an advantage over your spending.

Thinking about the bigger picture, the money and storage space that you save is going to allow you to make a smarter purchase in the future when it is necessary. Have you ever made a purchase and then saw something that you could've used more the following day? You either made the second purchase or felt bad that you could not get the item that you truly wanted. This type of situation is eliminated when you are able to prioritize the items that you buy. It is a small chance in your lifestyle that can lead to large rewards in the future.

As you practice your newfound skill, you will notice that you are less likely to become attached to temporary items. Once you have done your first big purge, you will realize how hard it can be to let go of certain things that you have become attached to through the years for no real reason. Your home should be like a revolving door that favors functionality. When you learn that you can let go of things that can eventually be replaced by new ones, you will feel less panic about letting go. Detachment is important in minimalism when you can apply it.

When you obtain a replacement item, you will know how to take better care of it so that it will last longer. This right here shows you how to feel gratitude for the things that you currently have. People with an abundance of items who are willing to buy new ones anytime they feel a whim are more likely to mistreat them. They aren't necessarily careless people, but they might not see the value in the items that they do have when they are constantly able to buy more. It is a humbling trait to possess, and it will help you effortlessly maintain your minimalism.

Maintaining Minimalism While Shopping

Practicing your new habits is going to take some effort, but you should be able to feel confident about your ability to only keep what you need in your home. When you go to a store, your old habits might threaten to kick in at first. It is natural for some people to become thrilled by the endless selection of items that are available in a store. Also, it becomes easier to be willing to believe in any gimmicks that come along with advertising. The following are some tips that you can practice when you are out shopping in order to ensure that you are shopping minimally:

- Take Inventory: Before you leave your home, take inventory on the things that you already have in abundance. Whether you are shopping for groceries or home goods, you will want to prevent yourself from buying things that you don't need just yet or at all. You don't need to write this all down but walk through your home in order to make a mental note. For example, if you are about to do your weekly food shopping, open the fridge for a few seconds to determine what you already have.

- Make a List: No matter where you are going, making a list is going to help you stay on track when you get to the store. Write down each item in order of importance to help you make the best decisions. You can start making your list as soon as you notice that you need to buy something, even if you are not about to go shopping. This helps you remember what you need to get. With the way that life can become busy, it is easy to forget about these things once you finally get to the store.

- Create a Budget: Minimalism promotes the idea of spending less money. Think about where you can shop for the things that you need and consider how much money you have to work with. Don't overestimate, or else you might be faced with inconveniences when your bills are due. The money that you use for shopping should be money that is currently readily available. Account for all of your expenses and consider how much you can safely spend after that. If you have $20 to buy groceries, you probably wouldn't want to opt for a health food store that carries only expensive options. This is the mentality that you should have as you decide where you need to shop.

- Beware of Deals: As we have already touched on, deals aren't always going to end up saving you money. Some 'deals' will actually convince you to buy things that you don't need. While you might be spending less at first, you will be going home with something that might not hold a purpose. If you think about it, you are still going to need to spend the money in the future anyway to get what you originally intended to buy.

- Shop Online: If you find yourself too tempted by the selection that you find in stores, you can consider making your purchase online. This works out well when you are only in need of a singular item. For example, you wouldn't need to go to a home goods store in order to purchase a new microwave. You could simply search for one online and make your purchase. The idea of browsing in a physical location can sometimes lead the way to temptation.

- Bring a Friend: Having someone with you as you shop who knows that you wish to follow a minimalist life can help you stay on track. Think about this person as an accountability buddy. If you get carried away or distracted, this person should be able to bring you back to your true reason for being at the store. Make sure that this is someone who you trust that has your best intentions in mind.

- Compare Prices: While you might think that you are finding the best price on an item, don't forget to compare prices. Certain brands might be just as effective, yet half the price! Comparison shopping is a great habit to pick up when you are making any kind of purchase. It is a way to be smart about how much money you are spending and how much value you are getting.

Chapter 8
Tips to Make Your Life More Efficient

"Conscienceless efficiency is no match for efficiency quickened by conscience." - Kelly Miller

Efficiency is one of the main elements of minimalism. Anyone can get rid of the items that they are no longer using, but it takes a truly efficient individual in order to maintain a great standard of living. The things that you are able to accomplish when you live minimally will show you how much you are able to rely on yourself. Starting from the instant that you wake up in the morning to what you do before your head hits the pillow at night, every action counts. Inaction counts even more. When you are doing nothing, you are actually creating a window for stagnant energy. In this window comes the possibility of distraction, delay, and failure. Even the strongest people face the challenge of trying not to become stagnant. In times of stress, the brain will grasp at anything that it can in order to try and get through them. Your goal is to train yourself to gravitate toward efficient actions. Think about ways that you can accomplish something, even when you have no resources to start off with.

To live an efficient life does not involve all work and no play; giving yourself free time to decompress is essential to avoiding stress. When everything around you is in working order, this becomes possible. The time that would ordinarily be spent taking care of the things that you have been procrastinating becomes the time that you can spend on yourself. Never feel ashamed to treat yourself to some self-care. This is important for your happiness and well-being. We all need it in our lives just as much as we need order and structure. This entire process becomes synonymous with the results that you will see. By considering the following tips, you will be able to feel great about the decisions you make and the success you will see.

Utilize Technology

- Store Passwords: When you have to log into a website, you will normally have a username and password to remember. In order to save time, consider storing your passwords in a safe location such as a password app. This type of app will make your internet browsing a lot faster while ensuring that you are always able to log into the websites that you need. Plus, when you have them stored in an app, you will not need to worry about having your passwords scattered on various notepads. This is one of the easiest ways to lose them or to compromise your security.

- Make Your Schedule Digital: You likely won't have the exact same schedule each week, so consider keeping track of it digitally. This is a way to keep it organized while also staying out of your way. You will have access to your schedule no matter where you are, at home, work, or out and about. When you know what you have planned ahead of time, you will be able to be adequately prepared for it. A big part of staying stress-free comes from being one step ahead of your responsibilities.

- Shop Online: For simple things that you must buy, consider purchasing them online. As mentioned, online shopping can be a great tool when you embark on a minimalist lifestyle. Not only will it take away the temptation of shopping in a physical location that is filled with an abundance of items, but it will also allow you to continue on with your life without missing a beat. Online shopping takes less than half the time that regular shopping does in most cases. Because you know exactly what you need to purchase, you will be more focused and organized.

- Set Reminders: No matter how organized you become, there is still a chance that you might forget some of your obligations. It happens to all of us, and it can cause great inconveniences in our lives. Using your phone, computer, or any other electronic device with the capability, set reminders for the most important things that you must do. These things normally have a deadline attached, so missing them would be a great hindrance. Allow technology to assist you by giving you the heads-up that you need.

- Read More: There is an endless selection of literature available at your fingertips. Education is something that can actually lead you to more productive and efficient behavior. Know that, at any time, you can do some research on the things that you are most curious about. Giving yourself this advantage is going to set you up for the best outcome. Also, reading for pleasure is a great way to unwind and relax. Letting your mind have a much-needed break is essential to be an efficient individual.

- Hire Someone: When you have a task that you truly do not feel you have time to accomplish, consider outsourcing. The internet is filled with countless resources for you to explore that allow you to hire someone for help. From cutting the lawn to painting the house, these are duties that you can outsource if necessary. Think about it as a way for you to give yourself a break. When you don't have to worry about these things, you can focus on other tasks ahead.

- Track Your Health: Many wonderful apps exist to ensure that you are maintaining your health. As much as living an efficient life is an important aspect of minimalism, so is taking care of yourself. Remember, without your physical health, you will not be able to complete the tasks at hand. These apps will remind you to do things such as drink enough water and get plenty of exercise. They can also allow you to track your calories or give you ideas for different healthy recipes that you can try.

Incorporate Organization

While we have already gone over the steps that are necessary toward organizing your home, you can also apply the concepts toward organizing your life. Scheduling is something that is very important to learn as a minimalist. Instead of spreading yourself thin by agreeing to everything on someone else's terms, you have the ability to create a schedule that works with your life. There are some things that cannot be altered, work for example. Your work schedule might be entirely inflexible, but that is okay. Create your schedule around the things that you cannot change. These things are considered mandatory, the things that you need to get done before accomplishing anything else.

The next level includes things that you must do but have flexible deadlines, doctor's appointments for examples. A doctor's appointment is essential, but you can schedule it for a time that works best for you. Instead of scheduling it during your lunch break which would involve you being in a rush or on a Saturday which is a day of free time, you can fit it in where it makes sense. An example would be an hour before you must go into work. This would involve you getting up a little bit earlier, yet not taking away any productive time from your day. Think about the way that you schedule these tasks in your life. Is there a way that you can make them more efficient simply by considering your other obligations?

For those tasks that require no deadline but are things that you would like to get done, make a set of goals for yourself. Creating your own deadline for the things that you can do on your own time is the best way to stay organized. When you give yourself too much freedom with these things, you might never get around to doing them. This is what normally happens when you attempt to purge your home for the first time. Decluttering doesn't necessarily require a deadline, but by setting one, you will be more likely to get it done faster. The key is to stay vigilant at all times. This will keep you focused on your goals.

Social interactions can also be more efficient when you consider the way that you organize them. Throwing a party the night before you have a big presentation due at the office is likely not going to result in your best performance. Consider scheduling it for a night where you do not have to get up early the following day. Small details like this will make your life easier. Instead of struggling to socialize as well as tend to your responsibilities, you will be able to do both effortlessly. Again, this all comes back to not spreading yourself thin. Many people believe that they have no choice but to do so. You always have a choice, and there is always a way to revamp your current schedule in order to make it more efficient.

Designate certain days for certain tasks. If you want to clean your house once a week, set a day that you plan on doing this regularly. This will eliminate the struggle of trying to figure out when you are going to accomplish it. Instead, you will know that the day you select is your cleaning day, and then you can organize your other events around this. The same can be said for days that you want to spend time with loved ones because social interaction is just as important as making sure that you are being productive. It takes balance in order to maintain an orderly lifestyle. If you have a few small but tedious tasks, try accomplishing them all in the same day. This way, you will only have to devote one day out of your week to them instead of working toward them every single day of the week. Small changes like this are going to show you how much happier you can be when living as a minimalist.

Make Final Decisions

The ability to make a decision is one that you should be proud of. It shows that you are able to consider the choices that you have in front of you while selecting the one that is going to work out the best for you. A trick to making better decisions involves making them final. When you say yes or no to something, practice the art of sticking with your choice. This allows you to promote more trust in yourself by teaching yourself that you know what is best for you. When you let other people make decisions for you, then you are surrendering your ability to live efficiently. While sometimes they might make choices that turn out well and in your favor, there might be other times when their choices cause you an inconvenience. You can avoid this from the beginning by making the choices yourself and ensuring that they are going to serve you as best as they can.

Saying maybe only increases the number of choices that you will be faced with. Maybe is merely a suggestion. Instead of defaulting to this type of a reaction, try to consider what would happen if you said yes or no. This provides you with a final choice so that you will not have to make a decision about the same thing again in the future. This is a great tool for avoiding procrastination. Being efficient encompasses all areas of your life. If you think about it, you are able to become more efficient at just about anything. From making a decision about cutting your hair to choosing between two job offers, practicing making final decisions is going to help you with your desire to live a minimalist life. The point is that you do not need to add any additional burdens on your to-do list. This list should only account for the tasks that will allow you to be the most productive version of yourself.

Remind yourself that making decisions does not make you a bad person. Sometimes, you will need to choose between two unfavorable options, but this is what makes you a strong person. Being able to see the good in each choice that you make is a great trait to have. It makes the negative things seem less bad and it will give you the ability to appreciate the good things even more. This is all part of growing as a person, and this is essentially what minimalism allows you to do. If you notice that you can become helpful in the decision-making process in someone else's life, take action if they ask for your input. You'd be surprised at how helping others can eventually lead you toward a path of helping yourself. When you do this, you are helping the other person grow.

Conclusion

Now you have learned the essentials on how to become a minimalist. As you have gathered, minimalism extends beyond your material items and actually aims to transform the way that you think and function. Through this newfound perspective, you are reducing your stress levels and building your productivity. All of this is done in order for you to live an efficient life. You must begin by decluttering your home. As there are many ways that you can approach this step, it is up to you to decide where you would like to begin. Taking a survey of the things that you own and the purposes that they serve is going to allow you to formulate a plan. This plan is going to keep you on track and organized.

You will then need to ask yourself what you need in order to live comfortably, differentiating between what is necessary and what is desired. There are no wrong answers for this step because it is entirely personal. A lot of factors in your life will shape the way that you define this question. Letting go is a big part of this process. You will likely be letting go of many items that you have been holding onto for some time. This can be difficult because of the attachment that you have likely developed with your material items. Know that you do have the ability to overcome this. Using rational thinking, understand that giving up the items that do not serve you, can actually lead to them being repurposed or reused.

For the things that you do keep, find a place to store each item. This will allow you to find them quickly and not have to worry about the stress involved with losing things. If you have certain items that work minimally, yet can still be used, consider if there is anything that you can do that will upgrade their purposes. Repurposing items that you keep is a great habit to form. Instead of simply replacing the item because you do not know what else to do, consider if there is any way that you can make it more efficient. Only replace items when they are broken or when you can truly use an upgrade.

The first big decluttering process is known as a purge. This is when you are likely going to be getting rid of the most items. Purging can be therapeutic in the sense that it will feel good to take items that are not being used out of your living space. Check-in with yourself every few months and consider if another purge must be done. As mentioned, this is not something that you will need to do every single week. You will likely only need to purge after the holidays because that is when most people obtain many new items at once. Through it all, allow yourself to feel at ease with this cleanse. You do not need to hold onto any guilt that might stem from purging. Know that if an item is no longer serving a purpose, then there is no reason that you need to hold onto it. Sentimental items are an exception. They add value to your life, therefore, they are serving a purpose.

Applying these techniques to your current lifestyle is all it takes in order to transform your current behaviors into minimalistic ones. You will find that you are happier and more carefree when you aren't worried about the burden of keeping too many items that do not serve a purpose in your life. The minimalism does not only apply to maintaining your physical space but also in the way that you plan and schedule events in your life. Your aim should be to create ease and efficiency through everything that you do. If there is a way to make a change in order to better serve this purpose, apply it and feel the satisfaction from living as a minimalist.

Bonus Material:

Book: Minimalism; Beginners Guide to Minimalism

"Less is more." - **Mies Van Der Rohe. 1886.**

Disadvantages of Dropshipping

Most of society today is under the impression that living a minimalist lifestyle means letting go of something physical. On the contrary, giving away your material possession is not all that minimalism is about. Minimalism is cutting out what is unnecessary in life, be it frivolous expenditure, meaningless social interactions or general negativity. Minimalism is about happiness in one's life and not about success. There is a time at when feels like fulfillment seems out of reach.

Minimalism may be able to chart out what areas of life are not at their best. Sometimes we are led to believe that specific things, usually physical belongings and property are the measures of happiness and contentment. This is a very negative way of going about life. We are led to believe that settling down and slowing down the adventurous spirit is what a mature person does, that taking care of one's responsibilities is what an adult is expected to do. But this is not entirely true. You can't just live your life paying bills and surviving. Going through life doing only what is expected is not the way to be a well-rounded human being. One must leave time to work on their mentality, platonic and romantic relationships and pursuing what is of benefit to your life.

Minimalism is now a trend that has been growing steadily over the years. It is believed to have roots within the Scandinavian people in Europe. The digital generation, the millennials have however popularized it. Most millennials have slowly realized that the economy is not what it used to be and are determined to live within their means. This has led to the adaptation of this less clustered way of life. Millennials are the group that has contributed to social and environmental awareness on the benefits of minimalism. Minimalism seeks to address consumerism and environmental issues using its philosophy of living with less. This trend is not just a trending hashtag on social media; it is a powerful movement that if adopted by everybody could change the world.

As we live in a consumerist society today, people have placed an unwarranted importance on material things and trends to maintain a false sense of importance and success. The age of the internet has given room for the rise of negativity and a shallow way of thinking. In this regard, keeping up with trends has led to the accumulation of many things, collections of makeup and closets filled with things that go out style within months. As minimalism is a journey, it helps to start by taking stock of the physical characteristics that are taking up space in our homes and removing them, opening up space for tranquility, because if you cannot feel peaceful in your own home, there is little point to the evaluation. We focus too much on the economy instead of looking at intrinsic values.

Reasons to Pursue Minimalism

As for the reasons to pursue a minimalist lifestyle, there are many, differing from person to person.

- One may include achieving goals sooner; Minimalists are more determined when pursuing their goals in school or life which is a positive impact of minimalism.

- Minimalists tend to stay away from television and social media. Their phones and computers are usually for work and occasional connection with friends and family. The space that would otherwise be used to mull over the internet will be free to be used more productively.

- Minimalists are calmer, having decluttered their minds of negativity. They have more peaceful thoughts and can be instrumental in deflating an explosive interaction and aid in mending broken relationships.

- By avoiding social media, a minimalist has more time for interpersonal relationships, particularly romantic relationships. You become more open when you spend quality time with your partner and you get to learn more about them.

- Minimalism allows an individual to opt out of options that will lead to debt. Less spending decreases the need for credit and smaller housing leads to fewer bills and mortgage costs are reduced significantly.

- Less time being worried about their own life allows a minimalist to see other people — their strengths, struggles, hardships and more. And with a more evolved emotional state, they can put themselves in other's shoes and assist where they can and reach out for encouragement.

- Minimalists can discover their purpose faster than other modern individuals. Having cut down on screen time and gone out into the world to see and experience what others have to offer as well as establishing strong interpersonal relationships, they can fulfill their lives and encourage and assist others reach the same level of fulfillment.

- Developing healthy friendships is essential to a minimalist. Having been able to discover who they are, they seek to make connections with people who can build on that while getting rid of those who seem to leech off of them. However, they also tend to maintain old friendships that persevered during hard times.

- Minimalists can utilize the little they have to fulfill their lives. They can overcome where others cannot see a way out.

- They can grow their talents to improve their own lives as well as that of others.

- Traveling is a breeze for minimalists. They tend to pack light and pick up what they need along the way. Their joy is not in what can be used to remember the visit but in the experiences themselves.

- They are punctual and tend to maintain good rapport with authority figures who can assist in their pursuit of accomplishment. Deadlines and appointments are adhered to religiously.

- Minimalists are less likely to fear failure as they are more confident in their abilities and have built rapport and gathered necessary connections through good relationships to see their vision accomplished.

- Having a clear mind allows minimalists to be less stressed.

- They tend to be empathetic. Being more involved in personal allows people to come to you with problems, and being a present friend, they are always willing to listen. This builds their friends trust and value.

- Minimalists tend to make friends faster. Their positivity attracts new people toward them and their willingness to be involved and engaged in the relationship keeps people interested.

- Minimalists tend to have a keen eye on the things that they need. Ridding their homes of clutter allows them to see what they need and can decide to get it based on this assessment.

- They are more innovative and can enter the entrepreneurship industry unhindered. Their confidence allows them to face the risks of starting a new venture and maximize their profits.

- Cutting back on unhealthy habits and finding time to exercise they can stay fit and healthy.

- They understand that it's the little things in life that bring the most happiness.

- Family relationships are meaningful, just as friends and romantic partners are. More time is made to grow these relationships, strengthen the bonds and spread to love to the younger generations.

- By building rapport among their professional colleagues, they can earn respect based off of their hard work and determination. They also assist those who are struggling to achieve their goals.

- Minimalism allows for a lot freer time which is one's to do with as they please. A lot of this is reinvested in work, relationships or adventure.

- For those who are environmentally conscious, there is no better way to live as you preach than to practice minimalism.

Understanding Minimalism

Minimalism may be an ongoing trend, with most people laughing it off as a fad that will be discarded as quickly as it was adopted, but there are clear benefits to decluttering your life. Most of these range from health to social and even your finances will thank you for this change. Of all the benefits that minimalism has to offer, mental benefits are more prominent. Their focus is increased exponentially when you are not always worrying about all the distractions that would be taking place otherwise. Productivity will shoot through the roof, and your work will be grateful for it. There can be much more to be accomplished by a focused mind.

Peace is achieved through both physical decluttering and mental decluttering. Tuning out the external noise allows one to be stress-free, enabling one to avoid triggers caused by triggering sensory organs. Avoiding stress enables one to avoid the numerous health conditions associated with it.

Once taking up a minimalist life, one can clearly define what it is they want and what it is they need. Cutting back on spending to achieve happiness allows for financial freedom enjoyable experiences. Sparing money with these kinds of purchases can allow one to travel and experience something they otherwise would not have been able to. Skip the presents on special occasions and opt instead for making unforgettable memories with people you love.

The increase in consumerism has negatively affected the environment, and climate change is evident. The more we buy, the greater the impact. A lot of what we buy impulsively or because it is rarely used and ultimately thrown out. Even the way these products are packaged is a cause for concern. Plastic is used for this, from packing materials from goods bought online to the containers in which take away food is delivered. Plastic is non-biodegradable, and that is a massive problem for the environment. The industries that manufacture these products need water, which is depleting the water reserves we have. They emit 60% of the greenhouse gases that are depleting the ozone layer. Companies are starting to feel the weight of production cost and are now using cheaper, readily available materials, which is causing cheap productions to flood the market. Minimalists tend to go for higher quality products which lasts longer thus reducing waste. They live in smaller homes which reduce energy consumption for light and heat. A minimalist uses fewer cleaning supplies. They spend less on home repairs and are virtually incapable of overconsumption, and they don't have space!

There are types of minimalists. There are three different ways in which minimalists wish to practice their lifestyle but follow the same simple foundation of a lifestyle centered on less.

- The aesthetic minimalist – they tend to care about aesthetics. It is not that they have less, but they indeed display very little of it. They tend to go for the simplest things, dull color, simple design, simple textures, and the likes.

- Essential minimalists – they like to challenge themselves to see how little they can survive off of. They buy less, use less and have only the most basic of requirements. They do not like to waste, so they will buy the best quality they can afford. If they can have only one thing, it should be the best.

- Experiential minimalists – these are the ones who seek adventure above everything else. They own very little just because they move around a lot and not because they had to throw things out. They are sometimes called "backpack" minimalist and are likely to want to learn new skills.

- Sustainable minimalists – they love the environment and are focused on cutting back things that bring harm to the environment. They will keep a lot of what is important if it means they don't have to go out and buy it. They aspire to live as green as is possible while making do. They will probably learn how to make what they need from scratch.

- Thrifty minimalists – they known as the sustainable types, but their goal is to spend as little as possible. They thrift for clothes and equipment and might even grow their food. They love tools that can multitask and will sometimes live with someone else to save rent. They can, however, be prone to holding on to things they consider important, so they don't have to buy it in the future.

- Mindful minimalists – they tend to use decluttering as a spiritual experience. They get rid of unnecessary things to let go of negative emotions like guilt or stress. It allows them to find inner peace and become better. They may read about spiritual decluttering.

For anyone looking to become a minimalist, there are a few suggestions on where to start. You can write down what it is you want to achieve by becoming a minimalist. They can serve as inspiration for when things get too tricky. They will help you stick to your transition. Get rid of anything you do not use or if you have a duplicate, toss it out too. Sometimes a simple technique helps to declutter. Put everything you don't need in a box and put it away for 30 days. If at the end of the month you don't remember what was in the box or didn't take anything out, give it away. Traveling light is another step. Try packing for two days if you are going away for four. If you need something, you will improvise. Gradually you will become more comfortable with traveling light. Try finding items of clothing that can be mixed and matched to create different looks thus decreasing your closet size. It has been known to make life easier. Try eating the same thing for each meal for a week. Rotate the choices and see how you like it. This goes a long way in making decisions about food. If you have ever found yourself needing money for an emergency, then you know how stressful it can be. Try setting a small amount of money as a savings goal. Save a little cash. Even if you are paying back a debt, do this anyway. When the goal is reached, you will have extra cash for a rainy day, and you will not be stressed about it.

All in all, minimalism allows one to promote what is important to them while removing other distractions. It seeks to avoid consumerism and eliminates the need to possess. Modern life is fast-paced and in that there is little chance to connect. And in a world that holds up a specific lifestyle as the gold standard, it is minimalism that provides an alternative way of living, a healthier way of living. Minimalists make a personal choice to live in this way. After achieving a minimalistic exterior, it allows for space to declutter the interior of our lives. Minimalism is accepted worldwide as a way of life, and there are quite some people who have successfully made the transition from modern life to a more subdued minimalist lifestyle.

Check out our Other *AMAZING* Titles!

1. Mind Hacking; Learn the Secrets to Change Your Mind to Positivity in 20 Days

Mind hacking means tapping into your mind's unlimited potential using self-discipline techniques. It could also mean to reach into the basic working of your brain or someone else's with the use of cryptic means.

Small Mind Hacks for Everyday Life

You can reduce the pain in your life just by using the power of your brain if you look at the wound from another end to make it seem smaller than it already is (you can always rewire your thinking process or how you perceive things. One can meditate and train their brain to feel less panicked about such painful situations). This can be done by using inverted binoculars. Similarly, when you are feeling pain, if you try to ignore it or make it seem smaller than it already is, it will reduce it. This can be done by looking from the wrong end of binoculars. On the other hand, focusing on pain makes us feel it more.

Unplanned things and scattered thoughts leave us frustrated and will likely lead to getting fewer thing done. When you function with a more organized thought process, you become more productive. Funnily enough, the best way to achieve this is by cleaning. You are probably not crazy about cleaning; however, having a clean workspace makes you much more efficient at dealing with tasks. One way to become more productive like this is by looking at your cluttered desk and imagining how it would look like if it was clean. Once you visualize it clean, you will already feel much better. Then, by keeping that image in your brain, you can easily work your way to making your desk cleaner. By comparing the clean and messy versions in your brain, you are telling your brain to automatically get started on the task at hand.

According to scientific research, raising your eyebrows and widening your eyes, as if you were curious or surprised can enhance your creative thinking.

When you write things down, you can remember them much easier. Writing down means physically with pen and paper, not typing them on your phone or computer. The reason for this is perhaps because some parts of your brains are linked to your hands. So, when you write it down, it becomes more vividly engraved in your brain than when you simply tell yourself to remember something.

If you have extreme nervousness and there are numerous aspects and exercises you can consider to avoid nervousness while performing certain tasks, such as singing. Singing keeps your brain occupied by giving it a task to do so it is unable to think about anything else. So, until you are done with a particular task, keep singing to yourself. Your brain can't stress about something if it's not focused on it, and it has to focus on the singing.

Laughter is truly the best medicine and another great way to relieve stress, as it releases dopamine. As you get older, it becomes more difficult to just laugh at anything. Also, after having a good laugh, you can think clearly. So, try to find entertainment that lifts your mood. A funny video or comedy show will surely do the trick.

The Brain as a Computer

A computer works on an input-output basis, and our brain follows this same procedure. It is not analog or digital. Our brain is like a computer and neurons are the transistors.

Our sensory organs produce stimuli which are carried to our nervous system where they are processed. Then, an appropriate response is generated.

However, cognitive scientists don't believe this to be the case. In any case, it is certainly not like a traditional computer. The following computational operations are seen in our nervous system.

1. The nervous system is an input-output system.

2. It generates a conscious experience, as we process the environment around us. It could be argued that computers cannot behave like this, but it can also be also argued that this is because computations haven't evolved to that point yet.

3. It produces feedback as a result of the environment.

4. It can give a response to the environment.

Computer-related terms are used to make us understand how the brain actually works. We use terms like long-term memory which is like the hard drive storage of a computer, as they are both used to store memory. The human thinking process is the same as the information processing that a computer does. This is not to imply that our brain works like a computer, but just to have an idea of how it really works. However, computers have unbiased rational thinking, while our thinking is driven by emotions.

Mental modification:

Thoughts are altered to give a person mental and physical strength to deal with a situation. Athletes and performers practice being in a state of extreme focus, which is called being "in the zone".

The brain accounts for about 2% of our body weight. However, it uses up to 25% glucose and 20% oxygen from our bloodstream. So, although it is a small organ, it still uses a lot of energy. (Science, 2019)[1]

Also, it is a myth that our brain stops growing when we reach adulthood. This has been disproven as our brain does make new connections. Also, there is proof that meditation can alter both the structure and function of the brain.

A positive attitude increases performance across all factors of our lives, whether it is our social lives, work, or school. A positive attitude boosts creativity, mood, and willpower and increases our productivity by as much as 31%. However, it often doesn't help in overall productivity of daily activities but can still add up to a positive point for mental modifications. to help us be more productive.

Your goals are not static, so when you think that being successful is going to ultimately bring success, that is where your downfall begins.

---

[1] Science, L. (2019). 10 Things You Didn't Know About the Brain. Retrieved from https://www.livescience.com/12916-10-facts-human-brain.html

You need to invest in the journey more than in the goal. By making yourself enjoy the process, you will be successful much quicker.

Being happy is not being brainwashed – it's a habit. It is not mindlessly repeating to yourself that you can do a task and that there is no need to worry about anything, because this way, what you are saying is different from what you are feeling. This is not positive thinking.

A positive outlook on life is developed deliberately. Like a habit, you need to be repeating it daily for it become a part of your mentality. When it does, it becomes an automatic response and you get to truly reap its countless benefits.

Mind Hacking for Positivity

Hacking your mind for positivity could be explained through a coding example. In a specific code, we write specific functions and use special keywords to execute whatever we want. Using this analogy, to hack your brain for positivity means to debug your negative emotions so that your brain works more smoothly and with a positive attitude. If you learn to control the functioning of your brain and to better regulate your thoughts and emotions, your mind will achieve inner peace.

Working with your brain will make your life much more efficient. If you can successfully program your brain to work with you, you can achieve much more and be much happier. However, like any new skill, you have to put time and effort into it.

Writing down and documenting your progress is extremely important, as it will speed up the mind hacking process. Generally, writing things down invokes repetition that reprograms our mind.

The following are some techniques you can try out to develop a positive attitude.

Acknowledge things that you are grateful for:

Take time out of your day to remind yourself and write down things for which you are truly grateful for. Try to write at least three things at a time. It can be about anything; from any simple thought to some new idea, just pour your thoughts onto the paper and let your thoughts flow.

Consciously sitting and thinking about positive things in your life will help you develop a healthier perspective. It will also deflect your thoughts from negative to positive because you are intentionally focusing on the good parts of life.

Once you are aware of the positivity around you, it's time to engage and contribute. Only then you will step inside the positivity circle of your life. It's time to give back positivity too. You can give a little thank you to any person that you frequently interact with or whose general presence uplifts your mood. Just imagine that you were the one receiving a thank you note; it would surely brighten up your day. Not only does it bring joy to them, but it will also put a smile on your face just thinking about this small yet meaningful act.

Every day, pick someone to be the subject of your thank you note, and let them know just how highly you think of them.

Exercise and Relaxation:

Exercise is not only beneficial to your mental and physical health; it will also make you happy. Your body becomes in better shape, and when you feel better about your body, you automatically become more positive.

Set aside some time to exercise. A daily walk of 20 minutes will do the trick. If you are determined to leave negativity behind, you have to find some time in your busy schedule.

Relaxing your mind through meditation can bring about very sound changes in your behavior and increase your positivity. It will help you gain semblance in your life. All the cluttered stress and negativity you take in every day could derail your mind into a spiral of distress and unhappiness. That is why you need to take time and sit by yourself every day and be alone with your thoughts. Just focus on your breathing and nothing else. A 15-minute meditation session is all you really need.

Smiling:

Smile to raise your level of happiness. When you smile, your brain senses that you are happy, and it will send you a signal to smile more, thus creating a smile loop. A smile loop can be created by thinking of a happy memory or by just grinning widely. When you do this, it can bring much more happiness and get you in a positive mindset. You can also use the smile loop when you are about to take on a hectic task.

Psychological Distance:

Psychological Distance and its benefits:

Construal level theory

In simple terms, psychological distance means taking a few steps back and looking at the bigger picture. It will allow you to step away from your current frame of mind and change your perspective about a situation. You will be able to analyze it from all angles and sides, and get a better gist at it. It will help you reach a solution and allow you to better deal with any situation at hand. Psychological distance is a powerful mind hack or exercise that can bring about the following advantages.

- Abstract mindset lessens the difficulty of the task at hand, and can make bigger, more complex problems easier to handle. When you feel overwhelmed by a task, try taking a mental break from your troubles and go back to them after a moment, and you will be in a much better mindset to take them on.

- Sometimes, you are surrounded by emotionally charged situations and you feel like the world is crumbling around you. It is better to distance yourself from those situations. Being in the middle of highly emotional situations for a long period of time can cause you a lot of stress. When you distance yourself, you can better think about and question the situation. Do not let yourself be sucked into highly emotional situations as this is detrimental to both your mental and physical health.

- Looking at the situation from an objective point of view will help you gain a broader perspective and will allow you to approach the situation from a different point of view. This will allow you to better deal with it and stave off any negativity that came along with it.

- You can better deal with emotional situations, especially those that elicit a negative response from you. If you imagine them shrinking or moving away, the negative emotions won't affect you as much. This is a great mind hack to fight off negative emotions that start to take root in your mind. Some of us sensitive folk are very easily affected by things that invoke emotion. It can cause distress and completely derail our thought process, so we need to learn how to deal with emotions.

- Psychological distance is a great way to be more yourself. In this hectic society, everyone tries to fit in, but they end up losing their way. If you are constantly in a secure, small frame of mind, you think and make choices based on it, and you are likely to give in to your social influences. If you follow everyone else, you will lose your own values. Psychological distance means thinking about ideas abstractly. If you think of the big picture, your thoughts roam free and give you an idea of your core values. You will find out what's truly important and what drives you. This will strengthen you individually and allow you to put your values before anything else.

- A big problem that creative people face is suffering from roadblocks in their creativity. Writers suffer writer's block and artists suffer art block. When this happens, you can't seem to formulate any good ideas, and when you do, it is not up to standard. People who aren't able to overcome this become distressed and sometimes so disheartened that they shut down their creative selves because they believe that they are not good enough. However, this creative roadblock is temporary, and Psychological distance is here to help you get out of it. You have to think of the task from a distance, as more creative insight is developed for tasks that we think are farther away from us. (Jia, Hirt & Karpen, 2009)[2]

- You will have better self-control. Those who tend to think about issues abstractly have said that they would rather have a delayed reaction to a situation than an immediate response. Abstract thinking will allow you to better evaluate situations and will allow you to come to a conclusion after thinking about it, rather than impulsively giving into whatever comes to your mind.

- Stepping back and looking at the bigger picture allows you to make rational and wise decisions. It is a pretty neat skill to have. If you want to always be calm and relaxed, this is the mindset that you need. You need to create a distance between your personal issues and yourself and need to understand them for what they truly are. When you step away from issues, you can do this objectively. You have to learn how they affect you and others around you, and when you learn to see the bigger picture in situations, you develop a fresh frame of mind. You must understand that things are not always in your control; once you do, you will gain a lot of peace and calmness.

Abstract thinking is not the ultimate solution, however, it helps to

---

[2] Jia, L., Hirt, E., & Karpen, S. (2009). Lessons from a Faraway land: The effect of spatial distance on creative cognition. Journal Of Experimental Social Psychology, 45(5), 1127-1131. doi: 10.1016/j.jesp.2009.05.015

broaden the way you think. It helps to broaden the way you think, but it can also make you feel like you understand a lot about the situation, when in reality, you are not really that aware. This is called the illusion of explanatory depth. If you always rely on abstract thinking, this is a drawback, and you have to find a balance between the both – illusion of explanatory depth and abstract thinking).

The Tetris Effect:

Negative feelings affect us a lot more than positive ones; in fact, they affect us almost three times more. (Support, 2019)[3]

Setbacks and negative ordeals tend to put a heavy dent on our motivation and creativity. Our brain focuses on the negative more than the positive. It is actually a protective mechanism. It may seem like our brain is wired to be negative, but the good news is that it can be wired for positivity, and by doing so, the possibilities are endless.

Tetris is a game that everyone knows. You fit different blocks together and a line disappears when all the blocks fill the row. The interesting thing is that when people were made to play this game as a part of the study, some participants reported having dreams of it, which meant that the brain was still making sense of it.

Playing the game also increases grey matter. The Tetris learning effect means that the brain consumes less energy as you become better at the game.

Neurons use synapses to let the brain make connections, and learning something new changes those connections. The more you utilize the

---

[3] Support, I. (2019). The Manager's Oath. Retrieved from http://blog.idonethis.com/the-managers-oath/

new circuit, the more your synaptic efficiency will increase. Connections will strengthen and become easier to access.

Doing a task over and over again will increase your brain efficiency for that specific task. You will use less brain power for it as you start to do it more often.

Now, apply this same idea to gain a positive attitude. When you start to actively look for positive influences and features in your life, you are using brain power over and over again to find happiness and positivity. If you can carry on doing this for a long time, it will be very easy for you to develop a positive outlook on life.

Want to read more? Check out our book on **Mind Hacking** *on amazon today!*

2. Declutter Your Mind; Your Daily Guide to Eliminate Stress, Stop Negative Thoughts and Anxiety Relief for a Happy Lifestyle

One of the things you see on TV more and more these days is advertisements for vitamins and supplements to help improve your mind. These ads usually promise to help improve your attention span, help increase concentration levels and even improve memory recall. While all of these things seem appealing, they point to a very disturbing trend. The fact is that more people are suffering from poor mental performance than ever before. While these vitamins and supplements may help to affect the symptoms of this epidemic, they don't address the actual cause. In short, the cause for poor mental performance, including stress, negative thinking, poor memory and lack of concentration, is a cluttered mind.

The real problem is that most people don't realize what the cause is. Thus, they simply address the symptoms and hope for the best. Only when you address the cause itself can you hope to eliminate the symptoms that plague you once and for all. The first step to addressing this issue is to understand how the mind works. One of the most accurate analogies for the mind is to think of it as a computer. Imagine that you are sitting at your computer trying to accomplish a particular task. If you only have one or two windows open, with no other tasks running in the background, then things will run smoothly. However, if you have a dozen windows open, and music playing in the background, as well as programs, downloading, then things will begin to go very wrong. At the least, the computer will take forever to do any one thing. Simply opening a webpage will be a true test of patience. At worst, things will begin to crash. Windows will freeze, programs will crash, and eventually, you will need to restart the computer just to get things working again.

This is what happens when you allow your mind to become cluttered. At first, things just begin to slow down. Your memory slips from time to time, but overall you are unconcerned. Then you begin to notice your focus isn't as sharp as it once was. Eventually, you find it hard to concentrate on even the most mundane of activities. After a while, you may even find that you simply have to stop and put everything down. You need to get some sleep, or you may even decide to take a few days off just to unwind. This is the same as having to shut down and reboot to get things to work again. The simple solution to this dilemma is to learn to run fewer programs at once simply. Just as you should limit how many windows and programs you run on your computer, so too you should learn to limit how much your mind is tasked with at any given time. This is critical if you want to prevent the crashing caused by overstretching your mental capacity.

While vitamins and supplements may help improve mental functions, they cannot replace the simple task of reducing the load on your mind. By limiting your mind to one or two functions at a time you increase your overall mental performance. Your memory focus and attention span all begin to increase as a result of your mind being able to provide more of those resources to each task you undertake. It comes down to simple math. Another way to envision this is to imagine having 100 apples. If you have 100 people to give those apples to, then each person gets one apple. However, if you have only ten people to give apples to, then each person gets ten apples. Your mind has only a finite amount of memory, focus, and attention to give at any given time. Thus, the more you have going on in your mind, the less of each it can give to each of those thoughts. However, if you can reduce the number of thoughts in your mind, then more memory, focus, and attention can be given to each.

All in all, the biggest benefit of having a clear mind is that you can increase your mental capacity. However, this is not the only benefit. The reduction of mental traffic in your mind will also help to reduce stress. Most of the stress we experience is the result of feeling stretched too thin. We often feel as though we are being pulled in all directions, is expected to give just a little more than we have. By limiting the directions, we are focusing on at any given time we reduce that feeling of being overstretched. This, in turn, helps to reduce our stress levels significantly. As stress is reduced, happiness begins to increase. This makes sense, seeing as happiness and stress are opposites, much like light and dark. The less you have of one is, the more you have of the other. Thus, by reducing the clutter in your mind, you will improve mental performance, reduce stress and achieve a state of mind that is more peaceful and happier overall.

Reasons We Hang on To Clutter

Emotional attachment to things is the main reason of mind cluttering. There are other main reasons for mind cluttering which are described below. It is common for people to hang on with their memories. Certain objects may provide a false sense of security. Sometimes we make ourselves feel secure and comfortable with the things which are emotionally attached to our thoughts. You collect things for many reasons. You think you will use it later, but the time never comes. Sometimes mind clutter happens when you are over committed. You do not know how to say no. You don't feel comfortable with anyone. This is due to mind cluttering. Always remember this your time is as valuable as anyone. Fear of failure causes mind cluttering. Like you don't want to lose some physical things which you liked the most. Are you being exhausted because your mind is stretched beyond its bounds? Perhaps you have a workload that is extremely difficult or maybe it's about a family crisis. If it is so, give yourself space to continue and handle the situation.

And there is another reason of mind clutter which is lack of time. Lack of time is always linked to another problem. It's also possible that you do not know how to make the most of your time, so it seems you do not have time. So always try to manage your time in a very good way.

Think out of the box so that you can change your life in a significant way. But often it comes from a perfectionist attitude, or what is called FOMU (Fear of Messing Up). It means that you spend a lot of time looking for solutions for your troubles without ever committing to someone because you're afraid you're going to make a mistake. The attitude of being perfect cannot keep the best of us for a very long time. It is better to act and learn from someone. Once you've identified the cause of junk in your mind, then you can work to prevent junk from the weather in your home. Keep in mind there may be several reasons; often this is the case. I know it would be easier if there was only one, but the multiple causes are usually linked in one way or another. By addressing one, you will most probably address everyone.

Almost everyone struggles with clutter. And everyone wants to get rid of it. Sprinkle thoughts, fears, and worries they all add to the spiritual mess. What can you achieve if all that spiritual space has been freed?

Are you focused and present, or are you mentally on your to-do list, thinking about e-mail answers, and debate? We wake up in the morning and watch our phones, read emails and news, checks the text messages and all the stuff like that. Then the rings begin. Someone is talking to you on Facebook. You want to thank the people for sharing your message on Twitter. You have a lot of Instagram holders. The car needs an oil change, the children need a haircut, and the dog has to clean his teeth at the vet. Have you already scheduled these plans? Do you have a grocery list? What is it for dinner? What did that man mean? Perhaps you should have ignored it. And then that project is at work - will it be done in time? Will this work? Will it be as good as the other one? Will your audience get it? We relive the past, we are worried about the future, and our administrative details leave our important ideas over, and we try to do everything right away. It does not work. Voices in your head will not be silent. It can feel very overwhelming, and our minds can be noised. Some of us even have voices of past experiences. We know we do not like it for a good reason. If the matter is in our control, do action. If it is not in our control, we only use energy to turn our wheels for nothing. All those things take so much space that there's hardly any room for the job you're supposed to do. Rubbish pulls us out of the current moment from the projects we work with and the people we work with. What if all that spiritual space is liberated? What if we get out to conquer that spiritual mess? What can we do with that spiritual space, instead? Here's what we would do: We will have more clarity and more focus. We can be more productive and efficient, and we want more bandwidth for creative breakthroughs. We will be less stressed and less likely to forget about details. But you can do something here. Look at nature. It goes with the flow. Water flows in the path of least resistance—fish swimming with the flow of the stream—they do not fight it. There are a time and place to climb that mountain and fight the difficult battle but be extremely selective about your mountains because they take almost all of your mental bandwidth if you do it right. Evaluate your options and do not allow it to ruin your mental real estate. We can sleep better without the conversations waking us up. We could focus on the important work, rather than distracted by the details.

Think that we are trying to remove each layer to reach the inner light bulb. This is what decluttering for the mind is. We need to kick back every thought, every concept, and every story which is unnecessary. We all experience moments of deep peace and love, clarity and connection. Those moments are the summary like the inner light bulb. Who does not want it? We spend so much time focused on the body, getting it in the right shape, and the right health. What we put in our mouths and how it affects our hips. We spend so much time focused on work, productivity and output. What we can do in a day and how it affects the bottom line. We spend so much time focused on other people, how they help or hinder us

The ultimate goal of deconstruction is clarity and peace. It is with clarity and peace that we move with ease, excitement, and freedom. We return to a state of innocence and presence, free from burdens of stigma, dogma, and drama that do not serve the realities of ours.

Letting Go

Why does your life get cluttered? This seems like a redundant question but forces you to reconsider whatever you have learned till now. Physical clustering is a result of our accumulation of material things. You hoard broken furniture in the hope that one day you will set it right, stockpile old sox, clothes, cosmetic items which have outlived their useful life, preserve discount coupons which have long expired, retain movie tickets of movies which you have seen and forgotten, and a lot of other stuff which seems to have sentimental value. This is the physical clutter which you live with.

What about the more dangerous and subversive mental clutter? You remember and regret a fight which you had with your mother twenty years ago, you reminisce and feel sad about a spat with your best friend in school which happened decades back, you recall a highly charged break-up and wish you had not behaved the way you did. This is like hoarding old memories which give you pain and hurt.

Aren't you surprised that you still hold on to these sad memories? How do you expect to be creative and achieve success if your mind is filled with bad thoughts? You must have realized that it is tough to remove these toxic thoughts and declutter your mind.

You hold on to these noxious old memories because you are not letting go. You don't loosen your grip on the past. There is a feeling of revenge that you will get back at those people one day, you will show them who you are, you will knock them down with your success, blah, blah, blah. You go on pickling in your poisonous concoction made up of toxic memories.

What is letting go? Acceptance is one part of letting go. You are what you are, and you just shrug your shoulders, shake your head and move on. The more important part of letting go is forgiveness. You have to let go of the feeling of revenge. You won't get back, you won't show them, you won't knock them down with a heavy punch to their belly, and you won't carry grudges. Let go of the negativity and forgive others for real and imagined hurt they have caused. Do it now. Immediately. How does it feel? Don't you feel relieved as if a huge weight has been lifted from your mind? Forgiveness is a gentle magical want which can dispel the accumulated hate in your mind. This new free you will never again fall into the trance of revenge.

This is not to say that you will never experience rejection and spite from others. You should not be bothered by how others behave. People behave in such a toxic manner more because of ignorance and lack of awareness. You must forgive them unconditionally. Forgiveness means accepting others in spite of their shortcomings. Don't think that merely avoiding such people constitutes forgiveness – it doesn't. You must forgive willingly, consciously and with a joyful demeanor. This is true forgiveness. Once you embrace forgiveness, you will immediately experience immense and abundant joy. Your head will feel light and weightless. You will feel buoyant and lively. The clutter in your mind will disappear instantly.

Another aspect of letting go is compassion. It means understanding the pain and suffering of others. It also encompasses a desire to help others overcome their problems. How does this assist in decluttering your mind? Our mind assigns intentions and reasons for the behavior of others towards us. We do not realize that people have their problems which they are struggling to cope with. Most of the time, people don't hurt you intentionally. They are fighting with their mental demons, and you just happen to be a victim of their frustrations. Compassion means understanding the difficulties of others and providing a helping hand where possible. You will notice that the animosity which you had felt earlier melts away and is replaced with understanding. It elevates your mood and puts your mind in a state of happiness. Compassion acts not only like a balm to others but also as a medicine to soothe your mind. Forgiveness and compassion are qualities which takes you to a higher plane of consciousness. Your mind becomes free of impurities and clutter. It is ready to experience new and constructive ideas, prepared to explore the frontiers of joy and hopeful of a successful future.

Want to read more? Check out our book on **Declutter Your Mind** *on amazon today!*

References

3 things I still splurge on while paying off debt. (2018, March 18). Retrieved September 6, 2019, from https://www.frugal-millennial.com/3-things-i-still-splurge-on-even-while-paying-off-debt/

Babauta, L. (2018). Letting go of possessions: Zen habits. Retrieved September 6, 2019, from https://zenhabits.net/letgo-possessions/

Declutter quotes (26 quotes). (2019). Retrieved September 11, 2019, from https://www.goodreads.com/quotes/tag/declutter

Budget Dumpster. (9 May 2019). How to declutter your home: A ridiculously thorough guide. (2019, May 9). Retrieved September 6, 2019, from https://www.budgetdumpster.com/resources/how-to-declutter-your-home.php

McCray, L. (2013, June 19). Making memories last: the art of sentimental upcycling. Retrieved September 6, 2019, from https://blog.etsy.com/en/sentimental-objects/

Rose, K. (2019, March 2). What are the benefits of reuse? Retrieved September 6, 2019, from https://sciencing.com/benefits-reuse-4586.html

Sweatt, L. (2018, July 31). 17 beautifully simple quotes to channel your inner minimalist. Retrieved September 11, 2019, from https://www.success.com/17-beautifully-simple-quotes-to-channel-your-inner-minimalist/

Time #1 Reason for Shopping Online (2011, July 27). Retrieved September 11, 2019, from https://www.marketingcharts.com/uncategorized-18528

Young, S. (2018, January 30). 18 tricks to make new habits stick. Retrieved September 6, 2019, from https://www.lifehack.org/articles/featured/18-tricks-to-make-new-habits-stick.html

www.ingramcontent.com/pod-product-compliance
Lightning Source LLC
Chambersburg PA
CBHW030223170426
43194CB00007BA/840